Building Robust, Multi-Platform Applications

A Deep Dive into Python, C#, and the Latest Software Development Trends

THOMPSON CARTER

Table of Content

TABLE OF CONTENTS

Introduction

Building Robust, Multi-Platform Applications

In today's fast-paced digital world, **multi-platform applications** have become the cornerstone of modern software development. Developers are increasingly tasked with creating applications that run seamlessly on a variety of platforms—**web, desktop, and mobile**, across multiple operating systems such as **Windows, macOS, Linux, Android, and iOS**. The goal is to deliver a consistent user experience, optimize performance, and minimize development time, all while ensuring that the application remains maintainable and scalable.

This book, **"Building Robust, Multi-Platform Applications: A Deep Dive into Python, C#, and the Latest Software Development Trends"**, is your comprehensive guide to understanding the intricacies of developing high-quality, cross-platform applications. Whether you are a seasoned developer looking to expand your skillset or a newcomer eager to dive into the world of multi-platform development, this book provides the knowledge and practical tools you need to succeed.

Why Multi-Platform Development Matters

As technology advances, users expect **seamless experiences** across devices and platforms. They demand mobile applications that sync effortlessly with desktop versions, websites that work across multiple browsers, and tools that function reliably on different operating systems. This is where **multi-platform development** comes into play.

The goal of multi-platform development is simple: **write once, run anywhere**. However, achieving this is far from trivial. Different platforms have unique requirements and limitations, making it a challenge for developers to ensure that an application performs optimally on all target platforms. In addition, the need to **manage and integrate multiple codebases** for various platforms can increase complexity and lead to potential maintenance issues.

Python and C# as Cornerstones of Multi-Platform Development

In this book, we focus on two powerful programming languages, **Python** and **C#**, which are at the forefront of multi-platform development. These languages have evolved over the years, offering developers the flexibility and

17

performance they need to create modern applications that span multiple platforms.

- **Python**, with its vast ecosystem of libraries and frameworks, is a top choice for building backend services, **data-driven applications**, and **machine learning** models. Python is widely known for its ease of use and readability, making it an excellent choice for rapid development.

- **C#**, on the other hand, is a **robust, object-oriented language** designed for developing **enterprise-grade applications**, particularly for **Windows** and the **Microsoft ecosystem**. With the advent of **.NET Core** and **Xamarin**, C# has become an increasingly popular choice for building cross-platform applications, offering a powerful and unified framework for creating mobile, desktop, and web applications.

Together, Python and C# provide an incredibly versatile toolkit for modern software development. Whether you are building a **machine learning-powered web application**, a **cross-platform mobile app**, or a **high-performance enterprise solution**, these languages are up to the task.

A Practical Guide for Real-World Development

This book is more than just a theoretical exploration; it is a **practical guide** filled with real-world examples, case studies, and hands-on exercises that will help you **build actual multi-platform applications**. You will explore frameworks and technologies that enable the creation of cross-platform apps, such as **Flask, ASP.NET Core, Xamarin, Flutter,** and more. You will also learn how to optimize applications for performance, scale them in the cloud, and integrate the latest technologies like **AI, machine learning, and blockchain** into your projects.

Here's what you can expect from this book:

1. **Foundations of Multi-Platform Development** – Learn about the various approaches to cross-platform development and the advantages and challenges of each.

2. **Python and C# in Cross-Platform Development** – Dive deep into how Python and C# can be leveraged to build scalable, performant applications that work across multiple platforms.

3. **Practical Examples and Case Studies** – Explore real-world success stories of companies and projects

that have used Python and C# for multi-platform development.

4. **Best Practices for Optimizing Performance** – Understand how to identify and fix performance bottlenecks, optimize memory usage, and ensure efficient data handling across platforms.

5. **Advanced Topics** – Learn how to implement **AI-powered features**, leverage **cloud technologies**, and create **secure applications** with **authentication and encryption**.

6. **CI/CD and DevOps for Multi-Platform Applications** – Discover how to streamline development workflows, automate testing, and deploy applications seamlessly using **GitHub Actions, Jenkins, Docker**, and **Kubernetes**.

7. **Future of Multi-Platform Development** – Stay ahead of the curve with insights into emerging trends in **low-code/no-code development**, **AI-assisted coding**, and the **future of multi-platform technologies**.

Who This Book is For

This book is designed for developers who want to master the art of **building scalable, cross-platform applications** using

Python, C#, and the latest software development trends. Whether you're an experienced developer or just starting, the content is structured to help you progress from foundational concepts to advanced techniques.

- **Beginners** will benefit from the clear explanations, easy-to-follow examples, and practical exercises.
- **Intermediate and advanced developers** will find valuable insights into optimizing performance, leveraging cloud services, and incorporating cutting-edge technologies like AI and machine learning into multi-platform applications.

What You Will Achieve

By the end of this book, you will have a thorough understanding of how to:

- Build applications that run seamlessly across **multiple platforms** (Windows, macOS, Linux, Android, iOS).
- Utilize **Python and C#** for backend, desktop, mobile, and web application development.
- Implement **best practices** in **performance optimization**, **memory management**, and **security**.

- Automate your development processes with **CI/CD** pipelines and **DevOps practices**.
- Stay ahead in the industry by integrating emerging technologies like **AI, cloud computing**, and **blockchain** into your multi-platform applications.

Final Words

As the world of software development continues to evolve, mastering the art of **multi-platform development** will position you at the forefront of innovation. This book equips you with the skills, tools, and knowledge to **build robust, scalable applications** that cater to the diverse needs of modern users. Whether you're creating web applications, mobile apps, or enterprise solutions, the techniques and frameworks discussed will empower you to **create high-quality, future-proof software**.

Now, let's dive into the exciting world of multi-platform development and start building applications that will impact users worldwide!

Part 1

Fundamentals of Multi-Platform Development

CHAPTER 1

INTRODUCTION TO MULTI-PLATFORM DEVELOPMENT

1.1 Why Build Multi-Platform Applications?

- The growing need for cross-platform solutions in modern software development.
- Business advantages: Cost savings, wider audience reach, and improved efficiency.
- User experience benefits: Consistency across devices and operating systems.
- Common challenges and limitations of multi-platform development.

1.2 Overview of Python and C# in Cross-Platform Development

- **Python:**
    - Interpreted, high-level, and widely used for cross-platform applications.
    - Key libraries and frameworks (PyQt, Kivy, Flask, Django).
    - Strengths: Flexibility, simplicity, and strong community support.
- **C# and .NET Core:**

24

- o Designed for cross-platform applications with .NET Core.
- o Supports Windows, macOS, Linux, and mobile (via Xamarin/.NET MAUI).
- o Strengths: Performance, enterprise use, and modern features.

- **Comparing Python and C#:**
  - o When to use Python vs. C# in multi-platform development.
  - o Can they be used together? Real-world examples of hybrid applications.

1.3 Understanding Platform-Specific vs. Platform-Independent Code

- **Platform-Specific Development:**
  - o Applications tailored to specific operating systems (e.g., Windows, macOS, Linux, iOS, Android).
  - o Pros: Optimized performance and better integration with native features.
  - o Cons: Requires multiple codebases, increased maintenance costs.
- **Platform-Independent Development:**
  - o Code that runs seamlessly across different operating systems.

- o Achieved through frameworks like .NET Core, Python, and Java.
- o Pros: Reduced development effort, cost-effective, easier maintenance.
- o Cons: Potential performance trade-offs, limited access to platform-specific features.
- **Choosing the Right Approach for Your Project:**
  - o Factors to consider (target audience, performance needs, budget).
  - o Hybrid approaches and real-world case studies.

CHAPTER 2

SETTING UP YOUR DEVELOPMENT ENVIRONMENT

A well-configured development environment is essential for efficiency and productivity. This chapter covers the tools, installation steps, and best practices for managing dependencies in multi-platform development using Python and C#.

2.1 Choosing the Right Tools: IDEs, Compilers, and Libraries

Integrated Development Environments (IDEs) and Text Editors

- **For Python:**
    - PyCharm (Full-featured, best for large projects)
    - VS Code (Lightweight, flexible, supports extensions)
    - Jupyter Notebook (Best for data science and quick scripting)
- **For C#:**

- o Visual Studio (Best for .NET development, powerful debugging tools)
- o JetBrains Rider (Alternative to Visual Studio, fast performance)
- o VS Code (Lightweight, supports C# via extensions)

- **Cross-Language IDEs:**
  - o VS Code (Supports both Python and C#)
  - o IntelliJ IDEA (Good for Python, can work with C# via plugins)
  - o Eclipse with PyDev (Good for Java/Python development)

Compilers and Runtimes

- **Python:** Uses an interpreter (CPython, PyPy, or Jython for Java integration).
- **C#:** Requires .NET SDK (compiles C# code into Common Intermediate Language).

Key Libraries for Multi-Platform Development

- **Python:** PyQt (GUI), Flask (Web), Kivy (Mobile), Pandas (Data Processing).
- **C#:** .NET MAUI (GUI), ASP.NET Core (Web), Xamarin (Mobile).

28

- **Cross-Language Libraries:** gRPC, JSON.NET, and RestSharp (for API communication).

2.2 Installing and Configuring Python and C# for Cross-Platform Development

Installing Python

- Download and install Python from python.org.
- Add Python to system PATH for command-line access.
- Use `pip` for package management (`pip install numpy flask` etc.).

Installing .NET Core and C#

- Download and install .NET SDK from dotnet.microsoft.com.
- Verify installation with:

```sh

dotnet --version
```

- Install C# compiler and runtime with:

```sh
```

```
dotnet new console -o MyApp
```

Configuring VS Code for Python and C#

- Install **Python extension** for VS Code.
- Install **C# extension (OmniSharp)** for .NET development.
- Enable IntelliSense and debugging tools.

Version Control Setup (Git & GitHub/GitLab/Bitbucket)

- Install Git from git-scm.com.
- Set up a repository and push your code:

```sh

git init
git add .
git commit -m "Initial commit"
git push origin main
```

2.3 Managing Dependencies Effectively

Dependency Management in Python

- Use `pip` and virtual environments:

```sh
```

```
python -m venv myenv
source myenv/bin/activate    # On Windows:
myenv\Scripts\activate
pip install flask numpy
```

- Use `requirements.txt` to store dependencies:

```sh

pip freeze > requirements.txt
pip install -r requirements.txt
```

Dependency Management in C#

- Use NuGet for package management:

```sh

dotnet add package Newtonsoft.Json
```

- Use `.csproj` files to manage project dependencies.

Cross-Language Dependency Management

- Docker for containerized environments.
- Package managers like Conda (Python) and Chocolatey (Windows).
- Using `Makefile` or `Bash scripts` for multi-language projects.

31

This chapter provides a practical setup guide for a smooth development workflow. Would you like to include screenshots or additional sections?

CHAPTER 3

UNDERSTANDING CORE PROGRAMMING CONCEPTS IN PYTHON & C#

A strong foundation in programming principles is crucial for developing multi-platform applications. This chapter explores core concepts in Python and C#, highlighting their similarities and differences with real-world examples.

3.1 Variables, Data Types, and Control Structures

Variables and Data Types

Both Python and C# support various data types, but they handle typing differently:

Feature	Python	C#
Typing	Dynamically typed	Statically typed
Integer	`int`	`int`

33

Feature	Python	C#
Floating Point	`float`	`double, float`
Boolean	`bool` (`True` or `False`)	`bool` (`true` or `false`)
String	`str`	`string`
Lists/Arrays	`list, tuple`	`Array, List<T>`
Dictionaries	`dict`	`Dictionary<TKey, TValue>`

Python Example:

```python
python
```

```python
name = "Alice"    # String
age = 30          # Integer
height = 5.6      # Float
is_active = True  # Boolean

print(f"{name} is {age} years old and {height} ft tall.")
```

C# Example:

```csharp
csharp
```

```csharp
string name = "Alice";
```

```
int age = 30;
double height = 5.6;
bool isActive = true;

Console.WriteLine($"{name} is {age} years old and
{height} ft tall.");
```

Control Structures (Loops and Conditionals)

Control structures help in decision-making and looping.

Conditional Statements

Python:

python

```
age = 18
if age >= 18:
    print("You are an adult.")
else:
    print("You are a minor.")
```

C#:

csharp

```
int age = 18;
if (age >= 18)
{
    Console.WriteLine("You are an adult.");
}
```

```
else
{
    Console.WriteLine("You are a minor.");
}
```

Loops

For Loop in Python:

python

```python
for i in range(5):
    print(f"Iteration {i}")
```

For Loop in C#:

csharp

```csharp
for (int i = 0; i < 5; i++)
{
    Console.WriteLine($"Iteration {i}");
}
```

While Loop in Python:

python

```python
count = 0
while count < 5:
    print(count)
    count += 1
```

While Loop in C#:

csharp

```csharp
int count = 0;
```

```
while (count < 5)
{
    Console.WriteLine(count);
    count++;
}
```

3.2 Object-Oriented Programming (OOP) Fundamentals

Both Python and C# support **OOP principles**:

- **Encapsulation:** Restricting direct access to object properties.
- **Inheritance:** Creating a new class based on an existing one.
- **Polymorphism:** Allowing different classes to be used interchangeably.

Creating a Class and Object

Python:

```python
class Person:
    def __init__(self, name, age):
        self.name = name
        self.age = age

    def introduce(self):
```

37

```
        print(f"My name is {self.name} and I am
{self.age} years old.")

p = Person("Alice", 30)
p.introduce()
```

C#:

csharp

```
class Person
{
    public string Name;
    public int Age;

    public Person(string name, int age)
    {
        Name = name;
        Age = age;
    }

    public void Introduce()
    {
        Console.WriteLine($"My   name   is   {Name}
and I am {Age} years old.");
    }
}

Person p = new Person("Alice", 30);
p.Introduce();
```

Encapsulation (Using Private Variables)

Python:

```
python


class BankAccount:
    def __init__(self, balance):
        self.__balance = balance    # Private
variable

    def deposit(self, amount):
        self.__balance += amount
        print(f"New balance: {self.__balance}")

account = BankAccount(1000)
account.deposit(500)
```

C#:

```
csharp


class BankAccount
{
    private double balance;

    public BankAccount(double initialBalance)
    {
        balance = initialBalance;
    }

    public void Deposit(double amount)
```

```
    {
        balance += amount;
        Console.WriteLine($"New            balance:
{balance}");
    }
}


BankAccount account = new BankAccount(1000);
account.Deposit(500);
```

Inheritance (Extending a Class)

Python:

python

```python
class Employee(Person):
    def __init__(self, name, age, job_title):
        super().__init__(name, age)
        self.job_title = job_title

    def work(self):
        print(f"{self.name}  is  working  as  a
{self.job_title}")


e = Employee("Bob", 35, "Software Developer")
e.work()
```

C#:

csharp

```
class Employee : Person
{
    public string JobTitle;

    public Employee(string name, int age, string
jobTitle) : base(name, age)
    {
        JobTitle = jobTitle;
    }

    public void Work()
    {
        Console.WriteLine($"{Name} is working as
a {JobTitle}");
    }
}

Employee e = new Employee("Bob", 35, "Software
Developer");
e.Work();
```

3.3 Error Handling and Debugging

Errors can be classified as:

- **Syntax Errors** (Detected at compile time)
- **Runtime Errors** (Occur during execution)

41

- **Logical Errors** (Incorrect logic leading to unintended results)

Try-Except in Python

python

```python
try:
    x = int(input("Enter a number: "))
    result = 10 / x
    print(result)
except ZeroDivisionError:
    print("Cannot divide by zero!")
except ValueError:
    print("Invalid input! Enter a number.")
finally:
    print("Execution complete.")
```

Try-Catch in C#

csharp

```csharp
try
{
    Console.Write("Enter a number: ");
    int x = Convert.ToInt32(Console.ReadLine());
    int result = 10 / x;
    Console.WriteLine(result);
}
```

```
catch (DivideByZeroException)

{

    Console.WriteLine("Cannot divide by zero!");

}

catch (FormatException)

{

    Console.WriteLine("Invalid   input!   Enter   a
number.");

}

finally

{

    Console.WriteLine("Execution complete.");

}
```

Summary of Key Takeaways:

- **Python** is dynamically typed, whereas **C#** requires explicit types.

- Both languages support OOP with **classes, inheritance, and encapsulation**.

- **Error handling** prevents applications from crashing due to unexpected inputs.

- Control structures and loops work similarly in both languages, with minor syntax differences.

This chapter builds a strong programming foundation, making it easier to transition into **multi-platform application development**. Would you like additional topics or real-world case studies added?

Part 2

Cross-Platform Frameworks and Technologies

CHAPTER 4

CROSS-PLATFORM DEVELOPMENT STRATEGIES

Developing software that runs on multiple platforms requires careful planning and an understanding of different development approaches. This chapter explores **native, hybrid, and cross-platform solutions**, how to balance **performance and flexibility**, and the challenges of developing for different **operating systems**.

4.1 Native vs. Hybrid vs. Cross-Platform Solutions

When building applications, developers must decide whether to write **native code**, use a **hybrid framework**, or develop with a **cross-platform framework**. Each approach has trade-offs in terms of **performance, development speed, and maintenance**.

Native Development

- **Definition:** Applications are built specifically for one operating system using platform-specific languages and SDKs.
- **Technologies:**
  - **Android:** Java, Kotlin
  - **iOS:** Swift, Objective-C
  - **Windows:** C#, .NET
  - **macOS/Linux:** Swift, C++, Python
- **Pros:**
  - Best performance and responsiveness.
  - Full access to hardware (camera, sensors, GPS, etc.).
  - More optimized UI/UX experience.
- **Cons:**
  - Requires separate codebases for each platform.
  - Higher development cost and maintenance effort.

Example: Native Mobile Development

- Android app written in **Kotlin**
- iOS app written in **Swift**
- Windows desktop app written in **C# and .NET**

Hybrid Development

- **Definition:** Uses web technologies (HTML, CSS, JavaScript) wrapped in a native container.
- **Technologies:**
    - **Ionic** (Angular-based)
    - **Cordova** (Bridges web apps to mobile)
    - **Electron** (For desktop apps)
- **Pros:**
    - Faster development since a single codebase can be used across multiple platforms.
    - Easier updates (web-based).
- **Cons:**
    - Performance limitations compared to native apps.
    - UI inconsistencies and dependency on third-party plugins for hardware access.

Example: Hybrid Development

- **Ionic** app for mobile that uses web-based UI components.
- **Electron** app for desktop that runs in a web view.

Cross-Platform Development

- **Definition:** Uses a single programming language to generate near-native applications for multiple platforms.
- **Technologies:**

- o **.NET MAUI** (Successor to Xamarin)
- o **Flutter** (Google's UI toolkit)
- o **React Native** (JavaScript-based)
- o **Kivy** (Python-based)

- **Pros:**
  - o A single codebase for multiple platforms.
  - o Closer to native performance than hybrid solutions.
  - o Good balance between development speed and maintainability.

- **Cons:**
  - o Still not as fast as native solutions for resource-intensive applications.
  - o UI components may not behave exactly like native components.

Example: Cross-Platform Development

- A **Flutter** app written in **Dart** that runs on **iOS, Android, Web, and Desktop**.
- A **.NET MAUI** app written in **C#** that runs on **Windows, macOS, iOS, and Android**.

49

4.2 Choosing Between Performance and Flexibility

The choice between **native, hybrid, and cross-platform** depends on the specific requirements of the project.

Key Considerations

Factor	Native	Hybrid	Cross-Platform
Performance	Best (direct access to OS features)	Slower (runs in WebView)	Near-native (optimized frameworks)
Code Reusability	Low (separate codebases)	High (one codebase)	High (one codebase)
Development Speed	Slow (longer time for multiple platforms)	Fast (uses web tech)	Medium (depends on framework)
UI/UX	Best (native components)	Mixed (web UI elements)	Good (but may not be fully native)
Hardware Access	Full access	Limited (depends on plugins)	Partial (depends on framework)

50

Factor	Native	Hybrid	Cross-Platform
Maintenance Cost	High (separate maintenance)	Low (one codebase)	Moderate (one codebase with platform-specific tweaks)

When to Choose What?

- **Use Native Development when:**
    - Performance is critical (e.g., games, video editing apps).
    - Maximum device-specific feature access is needed.
    - You need deep integration with OS services (background tasks, sensors).
- **Use Hybrid Development when:**
    - Speed of development is more important than performance.
    - The app is simple and doesn't require heavy processing.
    - You already have web developers who can reuse skills.
- **Use Cross-Platform Development when:**
    - You want a balance between performance and code reusability.

- The app is relatively lightweight but still needs to feel native.
- You want faster iteration and lower maintenance cost.

4.3 How Different Operating Systems Impact Development

Each **operating system (OS)** has unique challenges for developers.

Mobile OS Differences (Android vs. iOS)

Feature	Android	iOS
Programming Languages	Java, Kotlin	Swift, Objective-C
UI Frameworks	Jetpack Compose, XML-based UI	SwiftUI, UIKit
App Store Process	More flexible	Strict approval process
Device Fragmentation	High (various screen sizes)	Low (few device variations)

- **Challenge:** Android supports thousands of devices, requiring responsive layouts.
- **Challenge:** iOS has stricter app store policies, making approvals slower.

Desktop OS Differences (Windows, macOS, Linux)

Feature	Windows	macOS	Linux
Preferred Language	C#, C++, Python	Swift, Objective-C, Python	C, Python, JavaScript
Package Management	MSI, EXE	DMG, PKG	APT, RPM, Snap
GUI Frameworks	WPF, WinForms, .NET MAUI	SwiftUI, Cocoa	GTK, Qt, wxWidgets
User Base	Enterprise & gaming	Creative professionals	Developers & engineers

- **Challenge:** Windows applications often integrate with legacy systems.
- **Challenge:** macOS requires additional notarization and security settings.
- **Challenge:** Linux has multiple distributions, making compatibility harder.

Final Thoughts: The Best Strategy for Your Project

- **If performance is a priority: Go native (Swift, Kotlin, C#).**
- **If you need quick development: Go hybrid (Ionic, Cordova, Electron).**
- **If you need a balance of both: Go cross-platform (.NET MAUI, Flutter, React Native).**

Real-world companies often **mix approaches**:

- **Facebook & Instagram:** Built using **React Native** for cross-platform flexibility.
- **Microsoft Teams:** Uses **.NET Core and React** for performance and scalability.
- **Uber:** Initially hybrid, later moved to native for better performance.

Summary of Key Takeaways:

Native apps = Best performance but require separate codebases.

Hybrid apps = Fast development but can have performance issues.

Cross-platform apps = Good balance, but not perfect for all use cases.

Different OS platforms have unique challenges, and the right choice depends on your application's goals.

This chapter builds a foundation for selecting the **best cross-platform strategy** before diving into specific frameworks in the next chapters. Would you like any real-world case studies added?

CHAPTER 5

INTRODUCTION TO .NET CORE AND C# FOR MULTI-PLATFORM DEVELOPMENT

.NET Core has revolutionized C# development by enabling cross-platform capabilities, allowing applications to run seamlessly on **Windows, macOS, and Linux**. In this chapter, we'll explore the **capabilities of .NET Core**, how to **write cross-platform code** in C#, and the fundamentals of **ASP.NET Core for web development**.

5.1 Overview of .NET Core and Its Capabilities

What is .NET Core?

.NET Core is a **lightweight, high-performance, and cross-platform** framework developed by Microsoft. It is the successor to the traditional .NET Framework and supports **desktop, web, mobile, cloud, and IoT applications**.

Key Features of .NET Core

Cross-Platform Support: Runs on Windows, macOS, and Linux.

High Performance: Optimized for modern cloud and web applications.

Open Source: Fully open-source and maintained by Microsoft and the community.

Modular and Lightweight: Uses **NuGet packages** to include only necessary components.

Containerization Support: Works well with **Docker** and **Kubernetes**.

Built-in Dependency Injection: Simplifies application design and management.

Microservices Ready: Supports **REST APIs and microservices** architecture.

.NET Core vs. .NET Framework

Feature	.NET Core	.NET Framework
Cross-Platform	Yes (Windows, macOS, Linux)	No (Windows only)

Feature	.NET Core	.NET Framework
Performance	Faster and more lightweight	Heavier and slower
Open Source	Yes	No
Microservices	Fully supported	Limited support
Future-Proof	Actively developed	Legacy technology

With the introduction of **.NET 5+**, Microsoft unified **.NET Core and .NET Framework** into a single platform, simply called **.NET**.

5.2 Writing Multi-Platform Code with .NET and C#

One of .NET Core's biggest advantages is **write once, run anywhere** capability. Below, we explore how to write **cross-platform code** in C#.

Setting Up a .NET Core Project

Step 1: Install .NET SDK

- Download from <u>dotnet.microsoft.com</u>.
- Verify installation:

```sh

```

```
dotnet --version
```

Step 2: Create a Console App

```sh

```

```
dotnet new console -o MyApp
cd MyApp
dotnet run
```

C# Code Example: Hello World

```csharp

```

```
using System;

class Program
{
    static void Main()
    {
        Console.WriteLine("Hello, .NET Core!");
    }
}
```

Step 3: Run the Application

```sh

```

```
dotnet run
```

Works on **Windows, macOS, and Linux** without modification.

Handling File System Differences in Multi-Platform Development

When writing **cross-platform** C# applications, you need to account for OS-specific behaviors:

Example: Using Path Separators Properly
csharp

```
using System;
using System.IO;

class Program
{
    static void Main()
    {
        string           filePath         =
Path.Combine(Environment.GetFolderPath(Environm
ent.SpecialFolder.MyDocuments), "file.txt");
        Console.WriteLine($"File           path:
{filePath}");
```

60

```
    }
}
```

Uses `Path.Combine` to ensure compatibility across Windows (\), macOS/Linux (/).

Building a Cross-Platform Library

To create a **reusable multi-platform library**, use a **.NET Standard Library**:

Step 1: Create a Class Library

sh

```
dotnet new classlib -o MyLibrary
cd MyLibrary
```

Step 2: Write Platform-Independent Code

csharp

```csharp
public class MathHelper
{
    public static int Add(int a, int b) => a + b;
}
```

Step 3: Publish for Different Platforms

sh

61

```
dotnet publish -c Release -r win-x64
dotnet publish -c Release -r linux-x64
dotnet publish -c Release -r osx-x64
```

Now your library can run on any OS!

5.3 Using ASP.NET Core for Web Applications

What is ASP.NET Core?

ASP.NET Core is a **modern, high-performance, open-source framework** for **web applications and APIs**. It provides **better scalability, speed, and flexibility** than traditional ASP.NET.

Key Features of ASP.NET Core

Cross-platform – Works on Windows, Linux, and macOS.
Microservices support – Ideal for REST APIs.
Razor Pages & MVC – Enables dynamic, responsive web apps.
Blazor – Develop full-stack web apps using **C# instead of JavaScript**.

Creating an ASP.NET Core Web Application

Step 1: Create a New Web App

```sh
```

```
dotnet new webapp -o MyWebApp
cd MyWebApp
dotnet run
```

Opens at **http://localhost:5000**.

Step 2: Basic ASP.NET Core Controller

```csharp
```

```csharp
using Microsoft.AspNetCore.Mvc;

[Route("api/[controller]")]
[ApiController]
public class HelloController : ControllerBase
{
    [HttpGet]
    public string Get()
    {
        return "Hello from ASP.NET Core!";
    }
}
```

Step 3: Running the API

```sh
```

63

```
dotnet run
```

Open browser → **http://localhost:5000/api/hello** → *"Hello from ASP.NET Core!"*

Deploying an ASP.NET Core App to the Cloud

Host on Microsoft Azure

```sh
az webapp create --name MyWebApp --resource-group
MyResourceGroup --plan MyAppServicePlan
```

Deploy to Docker Container

```sh
docker build -t myapp .
docker run -d -p 5000:5000 myapp
```

Real-World Use Cases of .NET Core

Cross-Platform Desktop Apps:

- **Example: Microsoft Teams** (Built with **.NET Core and Electron**).

Web APIs and Microservices:

- **Example: Stack Overflow API** (Runs on ASP.NET Core).

Cloud-Native Applications:

- **Example: Azure Functions** for serverless computing.

Blazor for Web Development:

- **Example: Blazor WebAssembly** replaces JavaScript with C#.

Final Thoughts: Why Use .NET Core for Cross-Platform Development?

.NET Core allows developers to write applications once and run them anywhere. ASP.NET Core is a powerful framework for building fast, scalable web applications. C# is versatile, enabling development for web, desktop, cloud, and even IoT.

Key Takeaways from this Chapter:

.NET Core is a **modern, fast, and cross-platform** development framework.
C# can be used to build multi-platform applications that run on **Windows, macOS, and Linux**.
ASP.NET Core is a high-performance framework for **web development and APIs**.

Next Chapter: We'll explore **Python's Role in Cross-Platform Development** and how it complements C# in multi-platform applications.

CHAPTER 6

PYTHON FOR CROSS-PLATFORM APPLICATIONS

Python is a highly flexible language that supports cross-platform development across **desktop, mobile, and web applications**. This chapter explores **key frameworks** for building cross-platform apps, Python's role in different environments, and how Python can **interoperate with C#** for hybrid applications.

6.1 Key Libraries and Frameworks for Cross-Platform Development

Python offers several powerful **frameworks** for cross-platform development in **GUI, mobile, and web applications**.

Graphical User Interface (GUI) Development

Framework	Use Case	Platforms	Best For
PyQt	Desktop applications	Windows, macOS, Linux	Feature-rich, professional apps
Kivy	Mobile & desktop apps	Windows, macOS, Linux, Android, iOS	Touch-based, lightweight apps
Tkinter	Simple UI apps	Windows, macOS, Linux	Built-in Python GUI framework

Example: PyQt Desktop App

```python
from PyQt5.QtWidgets import QApplication, QLabel, QWidget
import sys

app = QApplication(sys.argv)
window = QWidget()
window.setWindowTitle("Hello PyQt")
label = QLabel("Hello, world!", window)
window.show()
sys.exit(app.exec_())
```

Runs on Windows, macOS, and Linux.

Mobile Development with Python

Python is not traditionally used for mobile apps, but frameworks like **Kivy** and **BeeWare** make it possible.

Framework	Use Case	Platforms	Best For
Kivy	Native-like mobile & desktop apps	Windows, Linux, iOS	macOS, Android, UI-heavy apps, games
BeeWare (Toga)	Native mobile & desktop apps	Windows, Linux, iOS	macOS, Android, UI Apps that use native

Example: Kivy Mobile App

python

```
from kivy.app import App
from kivy.uix.button import Button

class MyApp(App):
    def build(self):
        return Button(text="Hello, Kivy!")

MyApp().run()
```

69

Runs on Android, iOS, Windows, macOS, and Linux.

Web Development with Python

Python is widely used for web applications, with **Flask** and **Django** being the most popular frameworks.

Framework	Use Case	Best For
Flask	Lightweight web apps	APIs, small projects
Django	Full-featured web apps	Large applications, CMS, eCommerce

Example: Flask Web App

```python

from flask import Flask

app = Flask(__name__)

@app.route('/')
def home():
    return "Hello, Flask!"

if __name__ == '__main__':
```

70

```
app.run(debug=True)
```

Runs on all platforms via a web browser.

6.2 Using Python for Desktop, Mobile, and Web Development

Python is versatile and can be used across different application types.

Application Type	Best Python Frameworks	Best For
Desktop Apps	PyQt, Kivy, Tkinter	Productivity tools, GUI-based apps
Mobile Apps	Kivy, BeeWare	Android/iOS applications
Web Apps	Flask, Django	Websites, APIs, full-stack apps
Embedded Systems	MicroPython	IoT, hardware interactions

71

Python in Desktop Development

- **Why use Python for desktop apps?**
    - Simple and quick UI development.
    - Great for automation and productivity tools.
- **Best choice: PyQt for professional applications, Tkinter for simple apps.**

Python in Mobile Development

- **Why use Python for mobile?**
    - Cross-platform capabilities.
    - Rapid prototyping.
- **Best choice: Kivy for touch-based apps, BeeWare for native UI.**

Python in Web Development

- **Why use Python for web apps?**
    - Powerful backend frameworks.
    - Easy API development with Flask and Django.
- **Best choice: Flask for lightweight applications, Django for full-stack apps.**

6.3 Interoperability Between Python and C#

Python and C# can be used together in hybrid applications, leveraging the strengths of both languages.

Why Combine Python and C#?

- **Python for data science, AI, automation**
- **C# for performance, UI-heavy applications**
- **Mix both using interoperability tools**

Integration Method	Use Case	Tools
Calling Python from C#	Using Python's AI, ML libraries in C# apps	Python.NET, IronPython
Calling C# from Python	Using C# for high-performance tasks	CLR Hosting, Python for .NET
REST API Communication	Connecting Python and C# apps via APIs	Flask/Django (Python) + ASP.NET (C#)

73

Calling Python from C#

Example: Running Python from C# Using Python.NET

csharp

```csharp
using Python.Runtime;

class Program
{
    static void Main()
    {
        PythonEngine.Initialize();
        using (Py.GIL())
        {
            dynamic np = Py.Import("numpy");
            dynamic result = np.sqrt(16);
            Console.WriteLine(result);
        }
        PythonEngine.Shutdown();
    }
}
```

Useful for integrating AI and ML models written in Python into C# applications.

Calling C# from Python

Example: Using Python to Execute a C# DLL

python

```
import clr
clr.AddReference("MyCSharpLibrary")

from MyCSharpLibrary import Calculator

calc = Calculator()
print(calc.Add(5, 10))
```

Allows using high-performance C# libraries in Python applications.

Creating a Python-C# Hybrid Web App

Python Flask Backend

python

```
from flask import Flask

app = Flask(__name__)

@app.route('/data')
def data():
    return {'message': 'Hello from Python'}
```

75

```python
if __name__ == '__main__':
    app.run(port=5001)
```

C# ASP.NET Frontend Consuming Python API

csharp

```csharp
using System;
using System.Net.Http;
using System.Threading.Tasks;

class Program
{
    static async Task Main()
    {
        HttpClient client = new HttpClient();
        string response = await
client.GetStringAsync("http://localhost:5001/da
ta");
        Console.WriteLine(response);
    }
}
```

Combining Flask (Python) for API logic and ASP.NET (C#) for frontend UI.

Real-World Use Cases of Python-C# Integration

Game Development: Unity (C#) + Python AI models.

Financial Applications: Python for analytics, C# for GUI apps.

IoT Systems: C# for device control, Python for data processing.

Machine Learning & AI: Python for AI models, C# for integrating them into enterprise software.

Final Thoughts: Why Use Python for Cross-Platform Development?

Python's frameworks allow easy development of desktop, mobile, and web applications. Interoperability with C# makes Python powerful for hybrid applications.

Python can be used for AI, automation, and backend logic in multi-platform systems.

Key Takeaways from this Chapter:

PyQt, Kivy, Flask, and Django are essential for Python-based cross-platform apps.

Python works across desktop, mobile, and web with the right frameworks.

Python and C# can be integrated for powerful hybrid applications.

Next Chapter: We explore **Developing Web Applications with Python and C#,** combining both languages to create **full-stack, multi-platform applications**.

Part 3

Building Multi-Platform Applications

CHAPTER 7

DEVELOPING WEB APPLICATIONS WITH PYTHON AND C#

Web development plays a crucial role in **multi-platform applications**, and Python and C# are two of the most powerful technologies for building **scalable, secure, and high-performance web applications**. In this chapter, we explore **full-stack development** using **Flask (Python) and ASP.NET Core (C#)**, how to create and integrate **REST APIs**, and the best security practices for web applications.

7.1 Full-Stack Development with Flask and ASP.NET Core

Python (Flask) and C# (ASP.NET Core) are often used together to build **scalable full-stack applications**. Here's how they compare:

Feature	Flask (Python)	ASP.NET Core (C#)
Type	Lightweight web framework	Full-featured web framework
Best For	Prototyping, APIs, small projects	Enterprise-grade applications
Performance	Fast, but not optimized for large-scale apps	High-performance, built for scalability
Security	Requires manual configuration	Built-in authentication & security tools

A **typical architecture** using Flask for the backend and ASP.NET Core for the frontend might look like this:

Flask (Python) Backend → Handles API logic
ASP.NET Core (C#) Frontend → UI and interaction
Database (PostgreSQL, MySQL, MongoDB) → Stores application data

---

Creating a Flask Backend

Flask is a **minimalistic web framework** that makes it easy to build RESTful APIs.

Step 1: Install Flask

sh

```
pip install flask
```

Step 2: Create a Simple API

python

```
from flask import Flask, jsonify

app = Flask(__name__)

@app.route('/api/message', methods=['GET'])
def get_message():
    return jsonify({"message": "Hello from Flask
Backend!"})

if __name__ == '__main__':
    app.run(debug=True, port=5001)
```

Runs on `http://localhost:5001/api/message`

Creating an ASP.NET Core Frontend

82

ASP.NET Core can serve as the frontend UI that consumes the Flask backend.

Step 1: Create a New ASP.NET Core Project

```sh

dotnet new web -o MyWebApp
cd MyWebApp
dotnet run
```

Step 2: Call Flask API from ASP.NET Core

Modify `Program.cs` to call the Python API.

```csharp

using System;
using System.Net.Http;
using System.Threading.Tasks;

class Program
{
    static async Task Main()
    {
        HttpClient client = new HttpClient();
        string response = await client.GetStringAsync("http://localhost:5001/api/message");
        Console.WriteLine($"Response from Flask: {response}");
```

```
    }
}
```

ASP.NET Core frontend consuming Flask backend via REST API

7.2 REST APIs and Integrating Backend and Frontend

A **REST API** allows different applications to communicate. The backend **(Flask or ASP.NET Core)** exposes **endpoints,** while the frontend consumes them.

Building a REST API in Flask

```python
python

from flask import Flask, jsonify, request

app = Flask(__name__)

data = [{"id": 1, "name": "Alice"}, {"id": 2,
"name": "Bob"}]

@app.route('/api/users', methods=['GET'])
def get_users():
```

```python
    return jsonify(data)

@app.route('/api/users', methods=['POST'])
def add_user():
    new_user = request.json
    data.append(new_user)
    return jsonify({"message": "User added
successfully"}), 201

if __name__ == '__main__':
    app.run(port=5001)
```

API endpoints for retrieving and adding users

Consuming Flask API in ASP.NET Core

Modify `Program.cs` to **fetch and display** user data.

csharp

```csharp
using System;
using System.Net.Http;
using System.Text;
using System.Threading.Tasks;

class Program
{
```

```
static async Task Main()
{
    HttpClient client = new HttpClient();

    // Fetch Users
    string response = await
client.GetStringAsync("http://localhost:5001/ap
i/users");
    Console.WriteLine($"Users: {response}");

    // Add a new user
    var content = new
StringContent("{\"id\":3,
\"name\":\"Charlie\"}", Encoding.UTF8,
"application/json");
    await
client.PostAsync("http://localhost:5001/api/use
rs", content);
    Console.WriteLine("New user added!");
}
}
```

Now, ASP.NET Core can fetch and post data to Flask backend.

Integrating Flask Backend with an ASP.NET Core Web App

86

Use Flask as an API Server

- Runs on `http://localhost:5001`
- Provides endpoints for CRUD operations

Use ASP.NET Core for UI

- Calls Flask APIs to **fetch and display** data
- Renders the user interface

7.3 Security Best Practices for Web Applications

Security is a **critical** aspect of web applications. Whether using Flask or ASP.NET Core, developers should implement the following best practices:

Secure API Endpoints

- Use **JWT (JSON Web Tokens)** for authentication.
- **Python (Flask JWT Authentication)**

```python
from flask_jwt_extended import JWTManager,
create_access_token
```

```
app.config['JWT_SECRET_KEY']   =   'super-
secret-key'
jwt = JWTManager(app)

@app.route('/login', methods=['POST'])
def login():
    return
jsonify(access_token=create_access_token(
identity="user"))
```

- **C# (ASP.NET Core JWT Authentication)**

```csharp
csharp

services.AddAuthentication(JwtBearerDefau
lts.AuthenticationScheme)
    .AddJwtBearer(options =>
    {
        options.TokenValidationParameters
= new TokenValidationParameters
        {
            ValidateIssuerSigningKey    =
true,
            IssuerSigningKey    =    new
SymmetricSecurityKey(Encoding.UTF8.GetByt
es("super-secret-key")),
            ValidateIssuer = false,
            ValidateAudience = false
        };
    });
```

Secure Database Connections

- Use **ORMs** like SQLAlchemy (Python) or Entity Framework (C#) to prevent SQL Injection.
- **Use environment variables** instead of hardcoding credentials.

Example: Flask SQLAlchemy Connection (Safe)

```python
python

import os
from flask_sqlalchemy import SQLAlchemy

app.config['SQLALCHEMY_DATABASE_URI']       =
os.getenv('DATABASE_URL')
db = SQLAlchemy(app)
```

Protect Against CSRF (Cross-Site Request Forgery)

- **Enable CSRF Protection**
    - Flask: Use **Flask-WTF**
    - ASP.NET Core: Use **AntiForgeryToken**

Example: ASP.NET Core CSRF Protection

csharp

```
<form asp-action="SubmitData">
    @Html.AntiForgeryToken()
    <button type="submit">Submit</button>
</form>
```

Use HTTPS for Secure Communication

- **Flask:** Use `Flask-Talisman` to enforce HTTPS.
- **ASP.NET Core:** Configure `app.UseHttpsRedirection();`.

Example: Enforcing HTTPS in Flask

python

```
from flask_talisman import Talisman

app = Flask(__name__)
Talisman(app)
```

Example: Enforcing HTTPS in ASP.NET Core

csharp

```
app.UseHttpsRedirection();
```

Final Thoughts: Why Use Python and C# for Web Development?

Flask is lightweight and great for building APIs. ASP.NET Core provides high performance and enterprise-level   security. Combining both allows for scalable, multi-platform full-stack development.

Key Takeaways from This Chapter:

Flask (Python) is great for API backends, while ASP.NET Core (C#) is powerful for frontends. REST APIs allow communication between Python and C#   applications. Security best practices include authentication, database protection, CSRF prevention, and HTTPS enforcement.

Next Chapter: We dive into **Cross-Platform Desktop Applications with Python and C#**, building GUI-based apps with PyQt, Kivy, and .NET MAUI.

CHAPTER 8

BUILDING CROSS-PLATFORM DESKTOP APPLICATIONS

Cross-platform desktop applications allow developers to write code once and run it on **Windows, macOS, and Linux**. Python and C# provide powerful frameworks such as **PyQt, Kivy, and .NET MAUI** for building **graphical user interfaces (GUI)**. This chapter covers **GUI development**, **packaging and deployment**, and **performance optimization** techniques for desktop applications.

8.1 GUI Development with PyQt, Kivy, and .NET MAUI

Developers have several options when building **cross-platform desktop applications**:

Framework	Language	Best For	Platforms
PyQt	Python	Feature-rich desktop apps	Windows, macOS, Linux

Framework	Language	Best For	Platforms
Kivy	Python	Touch-based UI, mobile-friendly	Windows, macOS, Linux, Android, iOS
.NET MAUI	C#	Enterprise apps with native feel	Windows, macOS, Android, iOS

Developing a GUI with PyQt

PyQt is a Python binding for the **Qt framework**, making it powerful for creating **professional desktop applications**.

Step 1: Install PyQt

sh

```
pip install PyQt5
```

Step 2: Create a Basic PyQt Application

python

```
from PyQt5.QtWidgets import QApplication,
QLabel, QWidget
import sys

app = QApplication(sys.argv)
window = QWidget()
window.setWindowTitle("PyQt Application")
```

```
label = QLabel("Hello, PyQt!", window)
window.show()
sys.exit(app.exec_())
```

Runs on Windows, macOS, and Linux.

Developing a GUI with Kivy

Kivy is a Python framework for **multi-touch applications**, making it great for **cross-platform desktop and mobile apps**.

Step 1: Install Kivy
```
sh
```

```
pip install kivy
```
Step 2: Create a Basic Kivy Application
```
python
```

```
from kivy.app import App
from kivy.uix.button import Button

class MyApp(App):
    def build(self):
        return Button(text="Hello, Kivy!")

MyApp().run()
```

Works on Windows, macOS, Linux, Android, and iOS.

Developing a GUI with .NET MAUI

.NET MAUI (Multi-platform App UI) is the successor to **Xamarin.Forms**, allowing C# developers to build cross-platform applications with **native performance**.

Step 1: Install .NET MAUI

sh

```
dotnet new maui -n MyApp
cd MyApp
dotnet build
dotnet run
```

Step 2: Create a Simple UI in .NET MAUI (XAML-based UI)

Modify **MainPage.xaml**:

xml

```
<ContentPage
xmlns="http://schemas.microsoft.com/dotnet/2021
/maui"
```

```
xmlns:x="http://schemas.microsoft.com/winfx/200
9/xaml"
            x:Class="MyApp.MainPage">
    <VerticalStackLayout>
        <Label Text="Hello, .NET MAUI!" />
        <Button          Text="Click          Me!"
Clicked="OnButtonClick"/>
    </VerticalStackLayout>
</ContentPage>
```

Runs on Windows, macOS, iOS, and Android.

8.2 Packaging and Deploying Applications for Windows, macOS, and Linux

To distribute applications **without requiring the user to install dependencies**, developers must **package** them into **standalone executables**.

Packaging PyQt/Kivy Apps for Deployment

Platform Tool   Command

Windows pyinstaller pyinstaller --onefile app.py

96

Platform	Tool	Command
macOS	py2app	python setup.py py2app
Linux	pyinstaller	pyinstaller --onefile --noconsole app.py

Example: Creating a Standalone Windows Executable (EXE)

sh

```
pip install pyinstaller
pyinstaller --onefile --windowed myapp.py
```

Creates a **dist/myapp.exe** file.

Example: Packaging for macOS

sh

```
pip install py2app
python setup.py py2app
```

Creates a **macOS .app bundle**.

Packaging .NET MAUI Apps for Deployment

Platform Command

Platform	Command
Windows	`dotnet publish -c Release -r win-x64 --self-contained true`
macOS	`dotnet publish -c Release -r osx-x64 --self-contained true`
Linux	`dotnet publish -c Release -r linux-x64 --self-contained true`

Example: Publishing a .NET MAUI App for Windows

sh

```
dotnet publish -c Release -r win-x64 --self-contained true
```

Creates a **standalone executable** for Windows.

8.3 Performance Optimization Techniques

Optimizing desktop applications ensures **faster execution, lower memory usage, and better responsiveness**.

Optimize UI Performance

PyQt & Kivy: Use **lazy loading** for large datasets. **.NET MAUI:** Use **XAML UI virtualization** to render elements efficiently.

Reduce Application Startup Time

Use compiled bytecode instead of interpreting scripts every time.

- **Python:** Use `pyinstaller` to create optimized executables.
- **C#:** Use **Ahead-of-Time (AOT) Compilation** in .NET MAUI.

Enable AOT Compilation in .NET MAUI

Modify `csproj` file:

xml

```
<PropertyGroup>
    <PublishTrimmed>true</PublishTrimmed>
</PropertyGroup>
```

Optimize Memory Usage

Avoid memory leaks by properly handling objects.

- **Python:** Use `gc.collect()` to manually free up memory when needed.
- **C#:** Use `IDisposable` to properly clean up resources.

Example: Freeing Memory in C#

csharp

```csharp
using System;

class Program : IDisposable
{
    public void Dispose()
    {
        Console.WriteLine("Memory Released");
    }
}


static void Main()
{
    using (var p = new Program())
    {
        Console.WriteLine("Running...");
    }
}
```

Reduce Application Size

Exclude unnecessary files when packaging applications.

- **Python:** Use `pyinstaller --exclude-module unused_module app.py`.
- **.NET MAUI:** Use **trimming** to remove unused dependencies.

Optimize Database Performance

Use Indexed Databases for large data sets.

- **SQLite:** Works well for embedded databases.
- **PostgreSQL/MySQL:** Better for networked applications.

Example: Using SQLite in Python

```python
python
```

```python
import sqlite3
conn = sqlite3.connect('database.db')
cursor = conn.cursor()
cursor.execute("CREATE TABLE users (id INTEGER,
name TEXT)")
conn.commit()
conn.close()
```

Faster database operations with SQLite.

101

Final Thoughts: Why Use Python and C# for Cross-Platform Desktop Apps?

PyQt is great for feature-rich applications on Windows, macOS, and Linux.

Kivy enables cross-platform development for both desktop and mobile.

.NET MAUI is the best for high-performance, enterprise-grade apps.

Optimizing performance ensures fast execution, lower memory usage, and a better user experience.

Key Takeaways from This Chapter:

PyQt, Kivy, and .NET MAUI allow **cross-platform GUI development.**

Packaging tools like **PyInstaller, py2app, and .NET publish** help deploy applications.

Performance optimizations improve speed, memory usage, and application size.

Next Chapter: We dive into **Cross-Platform Mobile Development**, covering **Xamarin, Kivy, and React Native** for building mobile apps that run on Android and iOS.

CHAPTER 9

MOBILE APP DEVELOPMENT WITH PYTHON AND C#

Building **cross-platform mobile applications** allows developers to create apps that work seamlessly on **Android and iOS** without maintaining separate codebases. Python and C# offer powerful frameworks like **Kivy** and **Xamarin/.NET MAUI** for developing multi-platform mobile apps. In this chapter, we explore **how to build mobile apps using Kivy and Xamarin, handle device-specific features**, and **test and debug mobile applications** effectively.

9.1 Using Kivy and Xamarin for Cross-Platform Mobile Apps

Comparison of Kivy and Xamarin

Feature	Kivy (Python)	Xamarin/.NET MAUI (C#)
Platform Support	Android, iOS, Windows, macOS, Linux	Android, iOS, Windows, macOS
Language	Python	C#
Performance	Slower (uses OpenGL for UI)	Near-native (compiles to native code)
Best for	Lightweight, touch-based apps, rapid prototyping	Enterprise-grade apps with native UI
UI Framework	Custom UI (KV language)	Native UI (XAML-based UI)

Developing a Mobile App with Kivy (Python)

Kivy is a **Python-based framework** designed for **touchscreen applications**. It supports Android and iOS using **KivyMD** for material design components.

Step 1: Install Kivy

sh

105

```
pip install kivy
```

Step 2: Create a Simple Kivy App

```
python
```

```python
from kivy.app import App
from kivy.uix.button import Button

class MyApp(App):
    def build(self):
        return Button(text="Hello, Kivy!")

MyApp().run()
```

Runs on Windows, macOS, Linux, Android, and iOS.

Step 3: Build APK for Android

```
sh
```

```sh
pip install buildozer
buildozer init
buildozer -v android debug
```

Creates an **Android APK** for deployment.

Developing a Mobile App with Xamarin/.NET MAUI (C#)

Xamarin and **.NET MAUI** are **Microsoft-backed frameworks** for building **native-like cross-platform apps** with C#.

Step 1: Install .NET MAUI

```
sh
```

```
dotnet new maui -n MyMobileApp
cd MyMobileApp
dotnet build
dotnet run
```

Step 2: Create a Simple UI in .NET MAUI (XAML-based UI)

Modify **MainPage.xaml**:

```
xml
```

```xml
<ContentPage
xmlns="http://schemas.microsoft.com/dotnet/2021
/maui"

xmlns:x="http://schemas.microsoft.com/winfx/200
9/xaml"
            x:Class="MyMobileApp.MainPage">
    <VerticalStackLayout>
        <Label Text="Hello, .NET MAUI!" />
        <Button          Text="Click          Me!"
Clicked="OnButtonClick"/>
    </VerticalStackLayout>
```

```
</ContentPage>
```

Runs on Android, iOS, Windows, and macOS.

9.2 Handling Device-Specific Features

Different mobile platforms have **unique features** such as **camera, GPS, sensors, and notifications**. Cross-platform frameworks provide **APIs** to access these features.

Accessing Device Features in Kivy (Python)

Use **Pyjnius** (for Android) and **PyObjC** (for iOS) to access native device features.

Example: Accessing the Device Camera (Android)
python

```
from kivy.app import App
from           android.permissions           import
request_permissions, Permission
from plyer import camera

request_permissions([Permission.CAMERA])

class CameraApp(App):
    def build(self):
```

```
camera.take_picture('/storage/emulated/0/DCIM/t
est.jpg')
```

```
CameraApp().run()
```

Captures an image using the Android device camera.

Accessing Device Features in Xamarin/.NET MAUI (C#)

.NET MAUI provides built-in support for **platform-specific APIs**.

Example: Accessing the Device Camera

csharp

```
using Microsoft.Maui.ApplicationModel;
using Microsoft.Maui.Media;
using System.Threading.Tasks;

public async Task TakePhoto()
{
    var          photo          =          await
MediaPicker.CapturePhotoAsync();
    Console.WriteLine($"Photo      saved      at:
{photo.FullPath}");
```

109

}

Works on both Android and iOS without platform-specific modifications.

Example: Accessing GPS Location in .NET MAUI

csharp

```
using Microsoft.Maui.Devices.Sensors;
using System.Threading.Tasks;

public async Task GetLocation()
{
    var          location          =          await
Geolocation.GetLastKnownLocationAsync();
    Console.WriteLine($"Latitude:
{location.Latitude},                    Longitude:
{location.Longitude}");
}
```

Retrieves the current GPS location.

9.3 Testing and Debugging Mobile Applications

Testing ensures mobile apps work correctly across **different devices, screen sizes, and operating systems**.

Test Type	Purpose	Tools
Unit Testing	Tests individual functions	`unittest` (Python), `NUnit` (C#)
UI Testing	Ensures UI components function correctly	`Appium`, `XCTest`, `Espresso`
Performance Testing	Identifies slowdowns	`Profiler`, `Xcode Instruments`

Testing Kivy Mobile Apps

Step 1: Write a Unit Test in Python

```python
python

import unittest
from myapp import add_numbers

class TestMathOperations(unittest.TestCase):
    def test_addition(self):
        self.assertEqual(add_numbers(3, 2), 5)

if __name__ == "__main__":
    unittest.main()
```

Ensures functions return correct values.

Step 2: Use Appium for UI Testing

```sh
```

```
pip install Appium-Python-Client
```

Run Appium UI tests on Android/iOS.

Testing Xamarin/.NET MAUI Apps

Step 1: Write a Unit Test in C#

```csharp
```

```csharp
using NUnit.Framework;

[TestFixture]
public class MathTests
{
    [Test]
    public void AdditionTest()
    {
        Assert.AreEqual(5, 3 + 2);
    }
}
```

Ensures correct behavior of functions.

Step 2: Use Xamarin Test Cloud for UI Testing

```sh
sh
```

```
dotnet test
```

Runs tests in cloud-based device labs.

Final Thoughts: Why Use Python and C# for Cross-Platform Mobile Apps?

Kivy is great for lightweight mobile apps and quick prototyping.

Xamarin/.NET MAUI provides native-like performance and is enterprise-ready.

Handling device-specific features is easier in .NET MAUI, while **Kivy requires additional modules.**

Testing frameworks like NUnit and Appium ensure **apps run smoothly on real devices.**

Key Takeaways from This Chapter:

Kivy (Python) is good for rapid development, while Xamarin/.NET MAUI (C#) is best for performance-

heavy   mobile   apps. Device-specific features like camera and GPS can be accessed via Pyjnius (Python) or built-in .NET APIs (C#).

Testing ensures apps work correctly on multiple platforms.

Next Chapter: We explore **Cloud Computing and Integration in Multi-Platform Applications**, covering **AWS, Azure, and Firebase for mobile app backends**.

CHAPTER 10

INTEGRATING CLOUD COMPUTING IN MULTI-PLATFORM APPLICATIONS

Cloud computing enables **scalability, flexibility, and cost efficiency** for multi-platform applications. Whether you're building **web, desktop, or mobile applications**, integrating cloud services allows seamless data storage, authentication, real-time updates, and AI capabilities. This chapter covers **cloud services and deployment models**, how to **use Azure and AWS with Python and C#**, and an introduction to **serverless computing and microservices architecture**.

10.1 Cloud Services and Deployment Models

Types of Cloud Services

Cloud providers offer various services that developers can integrate into applications:

Service Type	Purpose	Examples
IaaS (Infrastructure as a Service)	Provides virtual machines, storage, and networking	AWS EC2, Azure Virtual Machines, Google Compute Engine
PaaS (Platform as a Service)	Provides a full development platform, including OS, runtime, and databases	AWS Elastic Beanstalk, Azure App Services, Google App Engine
SaaS (Software as a Service)	Fully managed software applications	Microsoft 365, Dropbox, Google Drive
BaaS (Backend as a Service)	Provides authentication, databases, and APIs for apps	Firebase, AWS Amplify, Azure Mobile Apps

Cloud Deployment Models

Deployment Model	Description	Use Case
Public Cloud	Hosted by third-party providers	General-purpose applications
Private Cloud	Dedicated for an organization	Banking, healthcare apps
Hybrid Cloud	Mix of public and private cloud	Enterprise applications
Multi-Cloud	Uses services from multiple cloud providers	Disaster recovery, high availability

10.2 Using Azure and AWS with Python and C#

Python and C# are widely used for cloud application development. **Azure** (by Microsoft) and **AWS** (by Amazon) provide comprehensive **cloud services**, including **computing, storage, databases, and AI integration**.

Deploying Python Applications to AWS

Step 1: Install AWS CLI and Boto3

sh

```
pip install boto3
```

Step 2: Upload Files to AWS S3

python

```
import boto3

s3 = boto3.client('s3')
s3.upload_file('localfile.txt',      'my-bucket',
'remote-file.txt')
```

Uploads files to an AWS S3 bucket.

Deploying C# Applications to Azure

Step 1: Install Azure CLI and SDK

sh

```
dotnet add package Azure.Storage.Blobs
```

Step 2: Upload Files to Azure Blob Storage

csharp

```
using Azure.Storage.Blobs;
using System;
using System.Threading.Tasks;
```

```
class Program
{
    static async Task Main()
    {
        string           connectionString       =
"your_azure_storage_connection_string";
        string containerName = "my-container";
        string filePath = "localfile.txt";

        BlobServiceClient  blobServiceClient  =
new BlobServiceClient(connectionString);
        BlobContainerClient   containerClient   =
blobServiceClient.GetBlobContainerClient(contai
nerName);
        BlobClient           blobClient          =
containerClient.GetBlobClient("remote-
file.txt");

        await blobClient.UploadAsync(filePath);
        Console.WriteLine("File           uploaded
successfully.");
    }
}
```

Stores files in Azure Blob Storage.

Deploying a Flask API to AWS Lambda (Serverless Computing)

AWS Lambda allows **serverless execution**, meaning you don't need to manage servers.

Step 1: Install AWS CLI & Serverless Framework

sh

```
pip install awscli
npm install -g serverless
```

Step 2: Write a Flask API

python

```
from flask import Flask, jsonify

app = Flask(__name__)

@app.route('/hello')
def hello():
    return jsonify({"message": "Hello from AWS Lambda!"})

if __name__ == '__main__':
    app.run()
```

Step 3: Deploy to AWS Lambda

sh

```
serverless deploy
```

Now, the API runs without managing a server.

Deploying an ASP.NET API to Azure Functions (Serverless Computing)

Step 1: Create an Azure Function App

```sh
sh
```

```sh
az functionapp create --resource-group
MyResourceGroup --consumption-plan-location
westus --name MyFunctionApp
```

Step 2: Write an ASP.NET Core API

```csharp
csharp
```

```csharp
using Microsoft.AspNetCore.Mvc;

[ApiController]
[Route("api")]
public class FunctionController : ControllerBase
{
    [HttpGet("hello")]
    public IActionResult Get() => Ok(new {
message = "Hello from Azure Function!" });
}
```

Step 3: Deploy to Azure

```sh
func azure functionapp publish MyFunctionApp
```

Now, the API runs in a fully serverless environment.

10.3 Serverless Computing and Microservices Architecture

What is Serverless Computing?

Serverless computing eliminates the need to manage infrastructure. Services like **AWS Lambda, Azure Functions, and Google Cloud Functions** automatically scale applications.

Feature	Benefits
Auto-scaling	Scales with user demand
Cost-efficient	Pay only for execution time
No infrastructure management	No need for manual server maintenance

Microservices Architecture

Microservices architecture breaks applications into **small, independent services** that communicate via APIs.

Feature	Benefits
Decentralized development	Teams can work on independent services
Scalability	Services scale independently
Improved tolerance	**fault** Failure of one service does not impact others

Building a Microservices-Based Web App with Python and C#

Flask for the User Authentication Microservice (Python)

python

```python
from flask import Flask, jsonify

app = Flask(__name__)
```

```python
@app.route('/auth/login')
def login():
    return jsonify({"message": "User logged
in"})


if __name__ == '__main__':
    app.run(port=5001)
```

Handles authentication for the app.

ASP.NET Core for the Product Microservice (C#)

```csharp
csharp

using Microsoft.AspNetCore.Mvc;

[ApiController]
[Route("products")]
public class ProductController : ControllerBase
{
    [HttpGet]
    public IActionResult Get() => Ok(new {
message = "List of Products" });
}
```

Handles product-related logic.

Deploying Microservices to Kubernetes (Cloud-Native Deployment)

sh

```
kubectl apply -f flask-auth.yaml
kubectl apply -f dotnet-product.yaml
```

Each microservice runs independently.

Final Thoughts: Why Use Cloud Computing for Multi-Platform Applications?

AWS and Azure enable scalable and flexible applications.

Serverless computing reduces infrastructure management overhead.

Microservices architecture improves scalability and fault tolerance.

Key Takeaways from This Chapter:

Cloud computing enhances the scalability of multi-platform applications. AWS and Azure provide easy-to-use cloud services for Python and C#. Serverless computing and microservices improve flexibility and cost-efficiency.

Next Chapter: We explore Database Management for Scalable Applications, covering SQL vs. NoSQL, performance optimization, and cloud-based databases.

Part 4

Advanced Topics in Software Development

CHAPTER 11

DATABASE MANAGEMENT FOR SCALABLE APPLICATIONS

Efficient database management is crucial for **scalable, high-performance multi-platform applications**. Whether handling **structured relational data (SQL)** or **flexible document-based storage (NoSQL)**, choosing the right database can impact performance, scalability, and ease of maintenance. In this chapter, we explore **SQL vs. NoSQL**, using **PostgreSQL, MongoDB, and SQLite** with **Python and C#**, and techniques for **optimizing database performance**.

11.1 SQL vs. NoSQL: Choosing the Right Database

Choosing between **SQL and NoSQL** depends on factors such as **data structure, scalability, and performance needs**.

Differences Between SQL and NoSQL

Feature	SQL Databases	NoSQL Databases
Data Structure	Relational (tables, rows, columns)	Non-relational (documents, key-value, graphs)
Scalability	Vertical (scale up by adding resources)	Horizontal (scale out by adding nodes)
Best For	Structured data (financial, transactional)	Unstructured data (real-time, IoT, social media)
Examples	PostgreSQL, MySQL, SQLite, SQL Server	MongoDB, Cassandra, Firebase, Redis

When to Use SQL?

Structured data with relationships (e.g., banking, inventory systems).

ACID compliance (Atomicity, Consistency, Isolation, Durability) for **strong consistency**.

Complex queries with joins and transactions.

When to Use NoSQL?

Unstructured, dynamic, or hierarchical data (e.g., social media, IoT).

Scalability and high availability (e.g., real-time applications).

Performance-intensive applications needing fast read/write speeds.

11.2 Using PostgreSQL, MongoDB, and SQLite with Python and C#

Python and C# support multiple databases. Here's how to integrate **PostgreSQL (SQL), MongoDB (NoSQL), and SQLite (lightweight SQL)** into applications.

Using PostgreSQL (Relational Database - SQL)

Setting Up PostgreSQL

- Install PostgreSQL: https://www.postgresql.org/download/
- Create a database:

```sql
CREATE DATABASE myapp;
```

Using PostgreSQL with Python (psycopg2)

```python
python

import psycopg2

conn = psycopg2.connect(
    dbname="myapp",                  user="postgres",
password="password", host="localhost"
)
cursor = conn.cursor()

cursor.execute("CREATE  TABLE  users  (id  SERIAL
PRIMARY KEY, name TEXT);")
cursor.execute("INSERT  INTO  users  (name)  VALUES
(%s);", ("Alice",))
conn.commit()

cursor.execute("SELECT * FROM users;")
print(cursor.fetchall())

conn.close()
```

Manages structured data with SQL queries.

Using PostgreSQL with C# (Entity Framework Core)

```csharp
csharp

using Microsoft.EntityFrameworkCore;
```

```
public class User
{
    public int Id { get; set; }
    public string Name { get; set; }
}

public class AppDbContext : DbContext
{
    public DbSet<User> Users { get; set; }

    protected                override               void
OnConfiguring(DbContextOptionsBuilder options)
        =>
options.UseNpgsql("Host=localhost;Database=myap
p;Username=postgres;Password=password");
}
```

C# with Entity Framework Core provides ORM-based database management.

Using MongoDB (Document-Based NoSQL Database)

Setting Up MongoDB

- Install   MongoDB:
  https://www.mongodb.com/try/download/community
- Start MongoDB server:

  sh

  mongod --dbpath /data/db

Using MongoDB with Python (PyMongo)

python

```
import pymongo

client                                      =
pymongo.MongoClient("mongodb://localhost:27017/
")
db = client["myapp"]
users = db["users"]

users.insert_one({"name": "Alice"})
print(list(users.find()))
```

Stores and retrieves flexible, schema-less data.

Using MongoDB with C# (MongoDB.Driver)

csharp

```csharp
using MongoDB.Bson;
using MongoDB.Driver;

var client = new
MongoClient("mongodb://localhost:27017");
var database = client.GetDatabase("myapp");
var users =
database.GetCollection<BsonDocument>("users");

var newUser = new BsonDocument { { "name",
"Alice" } };
users.InsertOne(newUser);

var allUsers = users.Find(new
BsonDocument()).ToList();
Console.WriteLine(allUsers);
```

MongoDB in C# supports high-speed, document-based storage.

Using SQLite (Lightweight SQL Database for Local Storage)

Using SQLite with Python (sqlite3)
```
python
```

```
import sqlite3

conn = sqlite3.connect("mydatabase.db")
cursor = conn.cursor()

cursor.execute("CREATE TABLE IF NOT EXISTS users
(id INTEGER PRIMARY KEY, name TEXT)")
cursor.execute("INSERT INTO users (name) VALUES
('Alice')")
conn.commit()

cursor.execute("SELECT * FROM users")
print(cursor.fetchall())

conn.close()
```

Ideal for local applications that don't require a full database server.

Using SQLite with C# (Entity Framework Core)

csharp

```csharp
using Microsoft.EntityFrameworkCore;

public class UserContext : DbContext
{
    public DbSet<User> Users { get; set; }
```

```
    protected          override          void
OnConfiguring(DbContextOptionsBuilder options)
        =>                options.UseSqlite("Data
Source=mydatabase.db");
}
```

Lightweight storage with full SQL capabilities.

11.3 Optimizing Database Performance

Efficient database management ensures **fast query execution and minimal latency**.

Indexing for Faster Queries

Indexes improve search speeds in both SQL and NoSQL databases.

SQL Example: Adding an Index
```sql
sql
```

```
CREATE INDEX idx_users_name ON users(name);
```

Reduces lookup times in large tables.

MongoDB Example: Indexing a Collection
```python
python
```

```
db.users.create_index([("name",
pymongo.ASCENDING)])
```

Speeds up searches in NoSQL databases.

Caching Frequently Used Queries

Caching prevents redundant database requests.

Using Redis for Caching in Python

```python
import redis

cache = redis.Redis(host="localhost", port=6379,
decode_responses=True)

cache.set("user_1", "Alice")
print(cache.get("user_1"))
```

Reduces load on the primary database.

Optimize Queries with Pagination

Fetching large datasets can slow down applications. Use **pagination** to load data in chunks.

SQL Pagination

```sql
sql
```

```sql
SELECT * FROM users LIMIT 10 OFFSET 20;
```

Retrieves data in smaller sets.

Connection Pooling for Efficient Resource Management

Keeping too many open connections slows down performance. Connection pooling allows efficient reuse.

PostgreSQL Connection Pooling in Python

```python
python
```

```python
from psycopg2 import pool

conn_pool = pool.SimpleConnectionPool(1, 10,
user="postgres", password="password",
database="myapp")
conn = conn_pool.getconn()
conn_pool.putconn(conn)
```

Prevents excessive connection creation overhead.

Final Thoughts: Why Database Optimization Matters for Scalable Applications?

Choosing SQL or NoSQL depends on data structure, performance, and scalability needs. PostgreSQL, MongoDB, and SQLite are widely used for different use cases. Indexing, caching, and connection pooling enhance database performance.

Key Takeaways from This Chapter:

Use SQL (PostgreSQL, SQLite) for structured, transactional data. Use NoSQL (MongoDB) for flexible, high-speed, schema-less storage. Optimize performance with indexing, caching, and pagination.

Next Chapter: We explore **APIs and Microservices Architecture**, covering **RESTful API design, microservices deployment, and inter-service communication.**

CHAPTER 12

APIS AND MICROSERVICES ARCHITECTURE

APIs and microservices architecture are essential for **scalable, maintainable, and cross-platform applications**. APIs allow **different applications to communicate**, while microservices break down a monolithic application into **independent, modular services**. In this chapter, we explore **designing scalable APIs with Flask (Python) and ASP.NET (C#)**, implementing **microservices**, and ensuring **API security and authentication**.

12.1 Designing Scalable APIs with Flask and ASP.NET

APIs (Application Programming Interfaces) allow **applications to exchange data**. The most common type is **REST (Representational State Transfer) APIs**, which use HTTP methods like **GET, POST, PUT, DELETE**.

Best Practices for Designing Scalable APIs

Use a consistent URL structure (`/api/v1/products`). **Support pagination and filtering** to handle large datasets. **Use proper HTTP status codes** (`200 OK`, `404 Not Found`, `500 Internal Server Error`). **Ensure security with authentication (JWT, OAuth).** **Document APIs with Swagger/OpenAPI** for better usability.

Building a REST API with Flask (Python)

Step 1: Install Flask

sh

```
pip install flask
```

Step 2: Create a Simple Flask API

python

```
from flask import Flask, jsonify, request

app = Flask(__name__)

products = [
    {"id": 1, "name": "Laptop"},
    {"id": 2, "name": "Smartphone"}
]
```

```
@app.route('/api/products', methods=['GET'])
def get_products():
    return jsonify(products)


@app.route('/api/products', methods=['POST'])
def add_product():
    new_product = request.json
    products.append(new_product)
    return     jsonify({"message":     "Product
added"}), 201


if __name__ == '__main__':
    app.run(debug=True)
```

Runs on `http://localhost:5000/api/products` and handles CRUD operations.

Building a REST API with ASP.NET Core (C#)

Step 1: Create an ASP.NET Web API Project

sh

```
dotnet new webapi -o MyWebAPI
cd MyWebAPI
dotnet run
```

Step 2: Create a Product API Controller

Modify `Controllers/ProductController.cs`:

csharp

```csharp
using Microsoft.AspNetCore.Mvc;
using System.Collections.Generic;

[Route("api/products")]
[ApiController]
public class ProductController : ControllerBase
{
    private static List<Product> products = new
List<Product>
    {
        new Product { Id = 1, Name = "Laptop" },
        new Product { Id = 2, Name = "Smartphone"
}
    };

    [HttpGet]
    public IActionResult GetProducts()
    {
        return Ok(products);
    }

    [HttpPost]
```

```
    public  IActionResult  AddProduct([FromBody]
Product product)
    {
        products.Add(product);
        return Created("", product);
    }
}

public class Product
{
    public int Id { get; set; }
    public string Name { get; set; }
}
```

Runs on `http://localhost:5000/api/products` and supports CRUD operations.

12.2 Implementing Microservices for Cross-Platform Development

What is Microservices Architecture?

Microservices break applications into **smaller, independent services**, each handling a **specific function**.

Feature	Benefits
Scalability	Each service scales independently
Flexibility	Use different technologies for different services
Fault Isolation	If one service fails, others keep running
Faster Deployment	Services can be updated separately

Example: Microservices-Based E-commerce App

Microservice	Function	Technology
User Service	Manages user authentication	Flask (Python)
Product Service	Handles product catalog	ASP.NET Core (C#)
Order Service	Processes orders	Flask (Python)
Payment Service	Manages transactions	ASP.NET Core (C#)

Deploying Flask and ASP.NET Microservices

Deploying a Flask Microservice (User Authentication Service)

python

```python
from flask import Flask, jsonify

app = Flask(__name__)

@app.route('/api/user/login', methods=['POST'])
def login():
    return jsonify({"message": "User logged in"})

if __name__ == '__main__':
    app.run(port=5001)
```

Runs on `http://localhost:5001/api/user/login`.

Deploying an ASP.NET Core Microservice (Product Service)

Modify `Program.cs`:

csharp

```csharp
var builder = WebApplication.CreateBuilder(args);
```

147

```
var app = builder.Build();

app.MapGet("/api/products", () => new[] { new {
Id = 1, Name = "Laptop" } });

app.Run();
```

Runs on `http://localhost:5002/api/products`.

Deploying Microservices with Docker

Create **Dockerfile for Flask Service**:

```
Dockerfile

FROM python:3.9
WORKDIR /app
 . .
RUN pip install flask
CMD ["python", "app.py"]
sh

docker build -t user-service .
docker run -p 5001:5001 user-service
```

Create **Dockerfile for ASP.NET Core Service**:

```
Dockerfile
```

```
FROM mcr.microsoft.com/dotnet/aspnet:6.0
. /app
WORKDIR /app
CMD ["dotnet", "MyWebAPI.dll"]
sh

docker build -t product-service .
docker run -p 5002:5002 product-service
```

Microservices now run in separate Docker containers.

12.3 API Security and Authentication

Securing APIs with JWT (JSON Web Token)

JWT ensures **only authenticated users can access APIs**.

Using JWT in Flask (Python)

```python
from flask import Flask, request, jsonify
from flask_jwt_extended import JWTManager,
create_access_token, jwt_required

app = Flask(__name__)
app.config["JWT_SECRET_KEY"] = "supersecret"
```

```
jwt = JWTManager(app)


@app.route('/login', methods=['POST'])
def login():
    token                                       =
create_access_token(identity="user1")
    return jsonify(access_token=token)


@app.route('/protected', methods=['GET'])
@jwt_required()
def protected():
    return jsonify(message="You have access")


if __name__ == '__main__':
    app.run()
```

Users must provide a valid JWT token to access /protected.

Using JWT in ASP.NET Core (C#)

Modify Program.cs:

csharp

```
using
Microsoft.AspNetCore.Authentication.JwtBearer;
using Microsoft.IdentityModel.Tokens;
```

```csharp
using System.Text;

var builder = WebApplication.CreateBuilder(args);
builder.Services.AddAuthentication(JwtBearerDef
aults.AuthenticationScheme)
    .AddJwtBearer(options =>
    {
        options.TokenValidationParameters = new
TokenValidationParameters
        {
            ValidateIssuerSigningKey = true,
            IssuerSigningKey = new
SymmetricSecurityKey(Encoding.UTF8.GetBytes("su
persecret")),
            ValidateIssuer = false,
            ValidateAudience = false
        };
    });

var app = builder.Build();
app.UseAuthentication();
app.UseAuthorization();
app.MapGet("/protected", () => "You have
access").RequireAuthorization();
app.Run();
```

Users must provide a JWT token to access /protected.

Protecting Against API Attacks

Security Measure	Prevention
Rate Limiting	Prevents API abuse
CORS Protection	Restricts cross-origin access
Input Validation	Prevents SQL injection
OAuth2	Secure authentication via third-party providers

Final Thoughts: Why APIs and Microservices Matter?

Microservices improve scalability and flexibility. Flask and ASP.NET Core are ideal for building scalable APIs.

Security measures like JWT protect APIs from unauthorized access.

Key Takeaways from This Chapter:

REST APIs enable seamless communication between applications.

Microservices architecture improves scalability and fault   tolerance.

Security best practices like JWT and OAuth2 protect APIs from threats.

Next Chapter: We explore **AI and Machine Learning Integration**, covering **how Python and C# can work with AI frameworks like TensorFlow and ML.NET**.

CHAPTER 13

AI AND MACHINE LEARNING INTEGRATION

Artificial Intelligence (AI) and Machine Learning (ML) are transforming **software applications**, enabling automation, predictive analytics, and intelligent decision-making. Python is a **leading language** for AI, with frameworks like **TensorFlow and Scikit-learn**, while C# is increasingly adopting **ML.NET** for AI integration. This chapter explores **machine learning in Python, AI in business applications**, and **real-world examples of AI-powered solutions**.

13.1 Machine Learning in Python with TensorFlow and Scikit-learn

Python is the **dominant language** for machine learning, thanks to its vast ecosystem of libraries.

Popular Python AI Frameworks

Framework	Use Case	Best For
TensorFlow	Deep Learning, Neural Networks	Image Recognition, NLP
Scikit-learn	Traditional ML models	Regression, Classification, Clustering
PyTorch	Research & production	Custom deep learning models
NLTK & SpaCy	Natural Language Processing (NLP)	Chatbots, Sentiment Analysis

Building a Machine Learning Model with Scikit-learn

Step 1: Install Scikit-learn

sh

```
pip install scikit-learn
```

Step 2: Train a Simple Classification Model

python

```
from sklearn.datasets import load_iris
```

155

```python
from sklearn.model_selection import train_test_split
from sklearn.ensemble import RandomForestClassifier
from sklearn.metrics import accuracy_score

# Load dataset
data = load_iris()
X_train, X_test, y_train, y_test = train_test_split(data.data, data.target, test_size=0.2)

# Train model
model = RandomForestClassifier()
model.fit(X_train, y_train)

# Make predictions
predictions = model.predict(X_test)
print("Accuracy:", accuracy_score(y_test, predictions))
```

Trains a simple classification model with 80% accuracy.

Building a Deep Learning Model with TensorFlow

Step 1: Install TensorFlow

sh

```
pip install tensorflow
```

Step 2: Train a Neural Network

```python
python

import tensorflow as tf
from tensorflow import keras
import numpy as np

# Generate sample data
X_train, y_train = np.random.rand(100, 5),
np.random.randint(2, size=100)

# Build a simple neural network
model = keras.Sequential([
    keras.layers.Dense(10, activation='relu'),
    keras.layers.Dense(1, activation='sigmoid')
])

model.compile(optimizer='adam',
loss='binary_crossentropy',
metrics=['accuracy'])

# Train the model
model.fit(X_train, y_train, epochs=5,
batch_size=10)
```

Trains a simple neural network for binary classification.

Using AI in C# with ML.NET

ML.NET is a **machine learning framework for .NET developers**, allowing AI integration into **C# applications**.

Step 1: Install ML.NET
```sh
sh
```

```sh
dotnet add package Microsoft.ML
```
Step 2: Train a Machine Learning Model in C#
```csharp
csharp
```

```csharp
using System;
using Microsoft.ML;
using Microsoft.ML.Data;

class HouseData
{
    public float Size { get; set; }
    public float Price { get; set; }
}

class Prediction
{
    [ColumnName("Score")]
    public float Price { get; set; }
}
```

```
class Program
{
    static void Main()
    {
        var context = new MLContext();

        // Sample data
        var data = new[]
        {
            new HouseData { Size = 1.1F, Price =
100000F },
            new HouseData { Size = 1.9F, Price =
200000F }
        };

        var            trainingData         =
context.Data.LoadFromEnumerable(data);
        var            pipeline             =
context.Transforms.Concatenate("Features",
"Size")

.Append(context.Regression.Trainers.Sdca(labelC
olumnName:  "Price",  maximumNumberOfIterations:
100));

        var model = pipeline.Fit(trainingData);
```

159

```
      var          predictionEngine       =
context.Model.CreatePredictionEngine<HouseData,
Prediction>(model);
      var           prediction         =
predictionEngine.Predict(new HouseData { Size =
2.5F });

      Console.WriteLine($"Predicted      Price:
{prediction.Price}");
   }
}
```

Predicts house prices using machine learning in C# with ML.NET.

13.2 Using AI in Business Applications

AI is widely adopted in **business applications** for **automation, efficiency, and data-driven decision-making**.

Common AI Use Cases in Business

Use Case	Technology	Industry
Fraud Detection	Machine Learning (Scikit-learn, ML.NET)	Banking, Finance
Customer Support Chatbots	NLP (TensorFlow, NLTK, SpaCy)	E-commerce, Tech Support
Predictive Analytics	Deep Learning (TensorFlow, PyTorch)	Retail, Marketing
Recommendation Systems	Collaborative Filtering (Scikit-learn)	Streaming, E-commerce
Medical Diagnosis	CNNs for Image Recognition (TensorFlow)	Healthcare

Example: AI for Fraud Detection in Banking

A **banking fraud detection system** can be built using machine learning to analyze transaction patterns.

Building a Fraud Detection Model in Python

python

```
import pandas as pd
```

161

```python
from sklearn.ensemble import IsolationForest

# Sample transaction data
data = pd.DataFrame({
    'amount': [100, 200, 5000, 50, 10000, 75,
300],
    'category': [1, 1, 2, 1, 2, 1, 1]
})

# Train fraud detection model
model = IsolationForest(contamination=0.2)
model.fit(data)

# Detect anomalies
data['fraud'] = model.predict(data)
print(data)
```

Detects fraudulent transactions based on anomalies.

13.3 Real-World Examples of AI-Powered Applications

AI is powering **real-world applications** across industries.

AI-Powered Personal Assistants

- **Google Assistant, Alexa, Siri** use **Natural Language Processing (NLP)** for voice recognition.

- **AI-powered chatbots** like **ChatGPT** enhance customer support.

AI in Healthcare: Medical Image Recognition

- **AI analyzes X-rays and MRI scans** for **early disease detection**.
- **Google's DeepMind** developed AI that outperforms radiologists in diagnosing breast cancer.

Building a Medical Image Classifier with TensorFlow

python

```
model = keras.Sequential([
    keras.layers.Conv2D(32,                  (3,3),
activation='relu', input_shape=(128,128,3)),
    keras.layers.MaxPooling2D(2,2),
    keras.layers.Flatten(),
    keras.layers.Dense(64, activation='relu'),
    keras.layers.Dense(1, activation='sigmoid')
])

model.compile(optimizer='adam',
loss='binary_crossentropy',
metrics=['accuracy'])
```

Trains an AI model for medical image recognition.

AI in E-commerce: Recommendation Engines

- **Amazon, Netflix, and Spotify** use AI to suggest products, movies, and music.

Building a Product Recommendation Model

python

```python
from sklearn.neighbors import NearestNeighbors
import numpy as np

# Sample product dataset
products = np.array([
    [100, 5],   # (price, rating)
    [150, 4],
    [200, 5],
    [500, 3]
])

# Train recommendation model
model                                    =
NearestNeighbors(n_neighbors=1).fit(products)
similar = model.kneighbors([[120, 4.5]])    #
Recommend similar product

print(similar)
```

164

Finds similar products based on price and rating.

Final Thoughts: Why AI is Essential for Modern Applications?

AI enhances automation, predictions, and decision-making.

Python is the best language for AI, while C# (ML.NET) is growing in adoption.

Machine learning improves fraud detection, chatbots, and healthcare.

Key Takeaways from This Chapter:

Python (TensorFlow, Scikit-learn) and C# (ML.NET) are powerful for AI.

AI is widely used in banking, healthcare, and e-commerce.

Real-world applications include chatbots, fraud detection, and recommendation engines.

Next Chapter: We explore **Cybersecurity and Secure Coding Practices**, covering **encryption, authentication, and common security vulnerabilities**.

CHAPTER 14

CYBERSECURITY AND SECURE CODING PRACTICES

Cybersecurity is **essential** in software development to protect **data, applications, and users** from cyber threats. This chapter explores **common security vulnerabilities**, techniques for **authentication and encryption**, and **security tools** to help developers build secure applications.

14.1 Common Security Vulnerabilities in Software Development

Many cyberattacks exploit weaknesses in software applications. Below are the most common vulnerabilities:

Top Software Security Vulnerabilities

Vulnerability	Description	Mitigation
SQL Injection	Attackers inject SQL commands into input	Use **parameterized queries** and ORM

Vulnerability	Description	Mitigation
	fields to manipulate the database.	(e.g., Entity Framework, SQLAlchemy).
Cross-Site Scripting (XSS)	Injects malicious scripts into web applications.	Sanitize and escape user input.
Cross-Site Request Forgery (CSRF)	Tricks users into executing unwanted actions.	Use **CSRF tokens** to validate user requests.
Broken Authentication	Poor authentication practices lead to account takeovers.	Use **multi-factor authentication (MFA)** and secure password policies.
Insecure APIs	Poorly secured APIs expose sensitive data.	Implement **OAuth2, JWT, and rate limiting**.

Example: SQL Injection Attack

An attacker inputs:

```sql
```

```
' OR 1=1; --
```

in a login form, which makes the SQL query always return **true**, bypassing authentication.

Vulnerable SQL Query:

```sql
SELECT * FROM users WHERE username = '" +
user_input + "';"
```

Secure SQL Query (Parameterized Query in Python with PostgreSQL):

```python
cursor.execute("SELECT * FROM users WHERE
username = %s;", (user_input,))
```

Prevents SQL injection by treating user input as data, not code.

14.2 Implementing Authentication and Encryption

Secure Authentication with JWT (JSON Web Token)

JWT is a secure token that authenticates API users.

Using JWT in Python (Flask)

python

```
from flask import Flask, jsonify, request
from flask_jwt_extended import JWTManager,
create_access_token, jwt_required

app = Flask(__name__)
app.config["JWT_SECRET_KEY"] = "supersecretkey"
jwt = JWTManager(app)

@app.route('/login', methods=['POST'])
def login():
    token                                    =
create_access_token(identity="user1")
    return jsonify(access_token=token)

@app.route('/protected', methods=['GET'])
@jwt_required()
def protected():
    return jsonify(message="You have access")
```

170

```python
if __name__ == '__main__':
    app.run()
```

Only authenticated users can access the protected route.

Using JWT in C# (ASP.NET Core)

Modify `Program.cs`:

csharp

```csharp
using
Microsoft.AspNetCore.Authentication.JwtBearer;
using Microsoft.IdentityModel.Tokens;
using System.Text;

var                  builder                  =
WebApplication.CreateBuilder(args);
builder.Services.AddAuthentication(JwtBearerDef
aults.AuthenticationScheme)
    .AddJwtBearer(options =>
    {
        options.TokenValidationParameters = new
TokenValidationParameters
        {
            ValidateIssuerSigningKey = true,
```

171

```
            IssuerSigningKey        =        new
SymmetricSecurityKey(Encoding.UTF8.GetBytes("su
persecretkey")),
            ValidateIssuer = false,
            ValidateAudience = false
        };
    });

var app = builder.Build();
app.UseAuthentication();
app.UseAuthorization();
app.MapGet("/protected",    ()    =>    "Access
Granted").RequireAuthorization();
app.Run();
```

Requires a JWT token for authentication.

Data Encryption with AES (Advanced Encryption Standard)

Encryption protects sensitive data by **converting plaintext into ciphertext**.

AES Encryption in Python

```python
python
```

```
from Crypto.Cipher import AES
```

172

```python
import base64

key = b"thisisaverysecurekey123"    # 16/24/32
bytes
cipher = AES.new(key, AES.MODE_EAX)
ciphertext,                tag              =
cipher.encrypt_and_digest(b"Sensitive Data")

print(base64.b64encode(ciphertext))
```

Encrypts data before storing or transmitting it.

AES Encryption in C#

csharp

```csharp
using System;
using System.Security.Cryptography;
using System.Text;

class Program
{
    static void Main()
    {
        string data = "Sensitive Data";
        using (Aes aes = Aes.Create())
        {
```

```
        aes.Key                      =
Encoding.UTF8.GetBytes("thisisaverysecurekey123
");
        aes.GenerateIV();
        ICryptoTransform      encryptor      =
aes.CreateEncryptor(aes.Key, aes.IV);
        byte[]            encrypted      =
encryptor.TransformFinalBlock(Encoding.UTF8.Get
Bytes(data), 0, data.Length);

Console.WriteLine(Convert.ToBase64String(encryp
ted));
        }
    }
}
```

Encrypts sensitive data before storage.

Secure API Requests with OAuth 2.0

OAuth 2.0 is a **widely used authentication framework** that allows users to log in securely.

OAuth2 in Flask with Google Login
```
python
```

```
from authlib.integrations.flask_client import
OAuth
from flask import Flask, redirect, url_for

app = Flask(__name__)
oauth = OAuth(app)
google = oauth.register(
    name='google',
    client_id="YOUR_CLIENT_ID",
    client_secret="YOUR_CLIENT_SECRET",

authorize_url="https://accounts.google.com/o/oa
uth2/auth",

access_token_url="https://oauth2.googleapis.com
/token",
    client_kwargs={"scope":    "openid    email
profile"}
)

@app.route('/')
def login():
    return
google.authorize_redirect(url_for('callback',
_external=True))

@app.route('/callback')
def callback():
    token = google.authorize_access_token()
```

```
    return token

if __name__ == '__main__':
    app.run()
```

Users can log in with Google instead of passwords.

14.3 Security Tools and Best Practices

Several tools help **detect and prevent vulnerabilities** in applications.

Security Tools for Developers

Tool	Purpose	Usage
OWASP ZAP	Scans web applications for vulnerabilities	Web application security testing
Burp Suite	Tests API security and intercepts requests	Web/API pentesting
SonarQube	Static code analysis for security issues	Code security scanning
Fail2Ban	Prevents brute-force attacks	Server security

Secure Coding Best Practices

Practice	Description
Use Least Privilege Principle	Limit user access to the minimum required.
Sanitize User Input	Prevents SQL injection and XSS attacks.
Use HTTPS Everywhere	Encrypts data during transmission.
Implement Strong Password Policies	Enforce complex passwords and MFA.
Perform Regular Security Audits	Use tools like OWASP ZAP and SonarQube.

Real-World Cybersecurity Case Study: Equifax Data Breach

In **2017**, Equifax suffered a **data breach exposing 147 million users** due to:

Unpatched Apache Struts vulnerability. Failure to encrypt sensitive data. Lack of multi-factor authentication (MFA).

Lessons learned: Keep software up to date (patch vulnerabilities). Use encryption for sensitive data. Implement MFA to prevent unauthorized access.

Final Thoughts: Why Cybersecurity is Critical in Software Development?

Security vulnerabilities can lead to data breaches and financial losses. Proper authentication (JWT, OAuth) prevents unauthorized access. Encryption (AES) ensures data security at rest and in transit. Security tools (OWASP ZAP, SonarQube) help detect vulnerabilities early.

Key Takeaways from This Chapter:

Secure coding practices protect against SQL Injection, XSS, and CSRF attacks. Use authentication methods like JWT and OAuth for secure access control. Encryption (AES) ensures data privacy and protection. Regular security testing and updates prevent breaches.

Next Chapter: We explore **Testing and Debugging Multi-Platform Applications**, covering **unit tests, integration testing, and debugging techniques.**

Part 5

Software Development Trends and Future Insights

CHAPTER 15

TESTING AND DEBUGGING

MULTI-PLATFORM

APPLICATIONS

Testing and debugging are **crucial** for building **reliable and maintainable** multi-platform applications. Whether developing for **desktop, mobile, or web**, a robust testing strategy ensures code quality and minimizes bugs. In this chapter, we cover **unit tests and integration tests**, **debugging techniques and tools**, and **automating testing processes** to enhance development efficiency.

15.1 Writing Unit Tests and Integration Tests

Software testing is categorized into **unit tests**, which check individual components, and **integration tests**, which verify interactions between modules.

Types of Software Tests

Test Type	Purpose	Example
Unit Test	Tests a single function/class in isolation.	Testing a `login()` function.
Integration Test	Ensures multiple modules work together.	Checking if `login()` interacts with a database.
Functional Test	Verifies the application works as expected.	Testing user login via UI.
End-to-End Test	Simulates real-world user interactions.	Checking a full checkout process in an e-commerce app.

Writing Unit Tests in Python (unittest and Pytest)

Install Pytest

```sh

pip install pytest
```

Unit Test Example: Testing a Calculator Function

```python

import unittest
```

```python
def add(a, b):
    return a + b


class TestCalculator(unittest.TestCase):
    def test_add(self):
        self.assertEqual(add(2, 3), 5)


if __name__ == "__main__":
    unittest.main()
```

Ensures that the `add()` function works correctly.

Run the Test

sh

```sh
python -m unittest test_calculator.py
```

Writing Unit Tests in C# (xUnit)

Install xUnit

sh

```sh
dotnet add package xunit
```

Unit Test Example: Testing a Calculator Class

csharp

```csharp
using Xunit;
```

```csharp
public class CalculatorTests
{
    [Fact]
    public void Add_TwoNumbers_ReturnsSum()
    {
        var result = Calculator.Add(2, 3);
        Assert.Equal(5, result);
    }
}
```

Validates the addition function using xUnit.

Run the Test

```sh
dotnet test
```

Writing Integration Tests in Python (Flask API Example)

```python
from flask import Flask, jsonify
import unittest

app = Flask(__name__)

@app.route('/hello')
```

```python
def hello():
    return jsonify({"message": "Hello, World!"})


class TestAPI(unittest.TestCase):
    def test_hello_endpoint(self):
        with app.test_client() as client:
            response = client.get('/hello')

self.assertEqual(response.status_code, 200)
            self.assertEqual(response.json,
{"message": "Hello, World!"})


if __name__ == "__main__":
    unittest.main()
```

Tests if the API endpoint /hello returns the expected response.

Writing Integration Tests in C# (ASP.NET API Example)

```csharp
csharp

using System.Net.Http;
using System.Threading.Tasks;
using Xunit;
```

```
public class APITests
{
    private readonly HttpClient _client = new
HttpClient();

    [Fact]
    public            async            Task
HelloEndpoint_ReturnsHelloWorld()
    {
        var     response     =     await
_client.GetAsync("http://localhost:5000/hello")
;
        var     content     =     await
response.Content.ReadAsStringAsync();
        Assert.Contains("Hello,        World!",
content);
    }
}
```

**Ensures that the API endpoint /hello returns the
expected response.**

15.2 Debugging Techniques and Tools

Debugging is an essential skill in software development.
Modern tools and techniques help identify and fix issues
efficiently.

Debugging in Python

Using print() for Debugging

python

```
def divide(a, b):
    print(f"Dividing {a} by {b}")
    return a / b

print(divide(10, 2))
```

Simple but effective for quick checks.

Using pdb (Python Debugger)

python

```
import pdb

def divide(a, b):
    pdb.set_trace()
    return a / b

print(divide(10, 2))
```

Runs an interactive debugger where you can inspect variables.

- Set breakpoints and inspect variables in **PyCharm**.
- Use **Step Over (F8)** and **Step Into (F7)** to navigate code execution.

Debugging in C#

Using Console.WriteLine() for Debugging

csharp

```
Console.WriteLine($"Dividing {a} by {b}");
```

Helps in quick debugging by printing values.

Using Visual Studio Debugger

- **Set breakpoints** in code.
- Use **Step Over (F10)** and **Step Into (F11)** for debugging.
- Watch variable values and check stack traces.

Using try-catch Blocks for Exception Handling

csharp

```
try
{
    int result = 10 / 0;
```

```
}
catch (DivideByZeroException ex)
{
    Console.WriteLine("Error: " + ex.Message);
}
```

Prevents application crashes due to runtime errors.

15.3 Automating Testing Processes

Automated testing improves development speed and ensures applications are continuously validated.

Setting Up a CI/CD Pipeline for Automated Testing

GitHub Actions for Python Testing

Create `.github/workflows/python-tests.yml`:

yaml

```
name: Python Tests
on: [push]
jobs:
  test:
    runs-on: ubuntu-latest
```

```
steps:
  - uses: actions/checkout@v3
  - name: Set up Python
    uses: actions/setup-python@v3
    with:
        python-version: "3.9"
  - name: Install dependencies
    run: pip install -r requirements.txt
  - name: Run tests
    run: pytest
```

Automatically runs Python tests on every push to GitHub.

GitHub Actions for C# Testing

Create `.github/workflows/dotnet-tests.yml`:

yaml

```
name: .NET Tests
on: [push]
jobs:
  build:
    runs-on: ubuntu-latest
    steps:
      - uses: actions/checkout@v3
      - name: Setup .NET
```

```
    uses: actions/setup-dotnet@v3
    with:
      dotnet-version: '6.0'
  - name: Install dependencies
    run: dotnet restore
  - name: Run tests
    run: dotnet test
```

Automatically runs .NET tests on every code commit.

Running Automated UI Tests with Selenium

Selenium automates browser testing for web applications.

Install Selenium for Python

sh

```
pip install selenium
```

Automated UI Test for a Webpage

python

```
from selenium import webdriver

driver = webdriver.Chrome()
driver.get("http://example.com")
assert "Example Domain" in driver.title
driver.quit()
```

Opens a web browser, checks page title, and closes it.

Final Thoughts: Why Testing and Debugging are Essential?

Unit tests catch early bugs and improve code reliability. Debugging tools like pdb (Python) and Visual Studio help diagnose issues. Automated testing with CI/CD ensures software quality in production.

Key Takeaways from This Chapter:

Unit and integration tests prevent regressions and errors.
Debugging tools like PyCharm and Visual Studio help troubleshoot issues.
CI/CD automation improves efficiency and reliability.

Next Chapter: We explore **DevOps and CI/CD for Multi-Platform Development**, covering **Docker, Kubernetes, and GitHub Actions for scalable software deployment.**

CHAPTER 16

DEVOPS AND CI/CD FOR MULTI-PLATFORM DEVELOPMENT

DevOps bridges the gap between **software development and IT operations**, ensuring that applications are built, tested, and deployed efficiently. **Continuous Integration and Deployment (CI/CD)** pipelines automate these processes, improving software quality and reducing time to market. In this chapter, we explore **CI/CD pipelines, GitHub Actions, Jenkins, Docker, and automated deployments**.

16.1 Continuous Integration and Deployment (CI/CD) Pipelines

What is CI/CD?

Continuous Integration (CI) → Automates testing and merging of new code.
Continuous Deployment (CD) → Automatically deploys tested code to production.

CI/CD Workflow Example

Developer pushes code to GitHub/GitLab. **CI server (Jenkins, GitHub Actions)** runs automated tests. **Docker builds a containerized application. CD deploys to a cloud environment (AWS, Azure, Kubernetes).**

Benefits of CI/CD

Benefit	Impact
Faster Development	Automates testing & deployment
Higher Code Quality	Ensures all code passes tests before merging
Early Bug Detection	Catches errors before production
Seamless Deployment	No downtime with rolling updates

16.2 Using GitHub Actions, Jenkins, and Docker

Setting Up CI/CD with GitHub Actions

GitHub Actions automates CI/CD workflows **directly from a GitHub repository**.

CI/CD Pipeline for Python Application

Create `.github/workflows/python-ci.yml`:

yaml

```
name: Python CI/CD
on: [push]
jobs:
  test:
    runs-on: ubuntu-latest
    steps:
      - uses: actions/checkout@v3
      - name: Set up Python
        uses: actions/setup-python@v3
        with:
          python-version: "3.9"
      - name: Install dependencies
        run: pip install -r requirements.txt
      - name: Run tests
        run: pytest
  deploy:
    needs: test
    runs-on: ubuntu-latest
    steps:
      - name: Deploy to Production
```

```
run: echo "Deploying to production..."
```

Runs tests and deploys only if all tests pass.

CI/CD Pipeline for C# Application

Create `.github/workflows/dotnet-ci.yml`:

yaml

```yaml
name: .NET CI/CD
on: [push]
jobs:
  build:
    runs-on: ubuntu-latest
    steps:
      - uses: actions/checkout@v3
      - name: Setup .NET
        uses: actions/setup-dotnet@v3
        with:
          dotnet-version: '6.0'
      - name: Install dependencies
        run: dotnet restore
      - name: Run tests
        run: dotnet test
  deploy:
    needs: build
    runs-on: ubuntu-latest
```

```
steps:
  - name: Deploy to Production
    run: echo "Deploying .NET App..."
```

Ensures only tested code gets deployed.

Setting Up CI/CD with Jenkins

Jenkins is an open-source CI/CD tool that automates builds and deployments.

Install Jenkins (on Ubuntu)

sh

```
sudo apt update
sudo apt install openjdk-11-jdk
wget -q -O - https://pkg.jenkins.io/debian-
stable/jenkins.io.key | sudo apt-key add -
sudo sh -c 'echo deb
http://pkg.jenkins.io/debian-stable binary/ >
/etc/apt/sources.list.d/jenkins.list'
sudo apt update
sudo apt install jenkins
```

Jenkins Pipeline for Python App

Create a Jenkinsfile:

197

```groovy
groovy

pipeline {
    agent any
    stages {
        stage('Build') {
            steps {
                sh 'python -m unittest discover'
            }
        }
        stage('Deploy') {
            steps {
                sh         'echo         "Deploying
Application..."'
            }
        }
    }
}
```

Executes automated tests and deploys the application.

Using Docker for CI/CD

Docker **packages applications into containers**, ensuring they run the same way on different platforms.

Dockerfile for a Flask Web Application

dockerfile

```
FROM python:3.9
WORKDIR /app
  .  .
RUN pip install -r requirements.txt
CMD ["python", "app.py"]
```

Build and Run the Docker Container

sh

```
docker build -t flask-app .
docker run -p 5000:5000 flask-app
```

Ensures the application runs in a consistent environment.

Deploying Docker Containers Using GitHub Actions

Step 1: Create docker-ci.yml

yaml

```
name: Docker CI/CD
on: [push]
jobs:
```

```
build:
  runs-on: ubuntu-latest
  steps:
    - uses: actions/checkout@v3
    - name: Build Docker Image
      run: docker build -t my-app .
    - name: Push to Docker Hub
      run: echo "${{ secrets.DOCKER_PASSWORD
}}" | docker login -u "${{
secrets.DOCKER_USERNAME }}" --password-stdin &&
docker tag my-app my-dockerhub-user/my-
app:latest && docker push my-dockerhub-user/my-
app:latest
  deploy:
    needs: build
    runs-on: ubuntu-latest
    steps:
      - name: Deploy Container
        run: docker run -p 5000:5000 my-
dockerhub-user/my-app:latest
```

Builds and deploys the Docker container automatically.

16.3 Automating Builds and Deployments

Automating Builds with Kubernetes

Kubernetes automates **scaling and deployment** of Docker containers.

Deploying a Flask App to Kubernetes

Create a Kubernetes Deployment (flask-app.yaml)

yaml

```
apiVersion: apps/v1
kind: Deployment
metadata:
  name: flask-app
spec:
  replicas: 2
  selector:
    matchLabels:
      app: flask-app
  template:
    metadata:
      labels:
        app: flask-app
    spec:
      containers:
        - name: flask-app
          image:          my-dockerhub-user/flask-
app:latest
          ports:
            - containerPort: 5000
```

Deploy to Kubernetes

sh

```
kubectl apply -f flask-app.yaml
```

Runs the application in a Kubernetes cluster.

Rolling Updates for Zero Downtime Deployment

A **Rolling Update** gradually replaces old containers with new ones.

Performing a Rolling Update in Kubernetes
sh

```
kubectl set image deployment/flask-app flask-app=my-dockerhub-user/flask-app:v2
```

Ensures zero-downtime deployment.

Final Thoughts: Why DevOps and CI/CD Matter?

CI/CD pipelines automate testing and deployment, reducing manual effort.

Docker ensures applications run consistently across environments.

Kubernetes enables automated scaling and rolling updates.

Key Takeaways from This Chapter:

CI/CD with GitHub Actions and Jenkins improves software   reliability.
Docker containers ensure cross-platform compatibility.
Automated deployments with Kubernetes enhance scalability.

Next Chapter: We explore **Blockchain and Smart Contracts**, covering **Ethereum, Solidity, and real-world blockchain applications**.

CHAPTER 17

PERFORMANCE OPTIMIZATION FOR CROSS-PLATFORM APPLICATIONS

Performance optimization ensures that **cross-platform applications** run efficiently across **Windows, macOS, Linux, Android, and iOS**. Poorly optimized applications lead to **slow execution, high memory usage, and poor user experience**. In this chapter, we explore **identifying and fixing performance bottlenecks, memory management in Python and C#**, and **load testing and stress testing**.

17.1 Identifying and Fixing Performance Bottlenecks

What is a Performance Bottleneck?

A bottleneck is any **resource constraint** (CPU, memory, disk, network) that slows down an application.

Common Bottlenecks in Multi-Platform Development

Bottleneck	Cause	Optimization
Slow Database Queries	Unindexed queries	Use indexing, caching
High CPU Usage	Inefficient loops, unnecessary calculations	Optimize algorithms, use threading
Memory Leaks	Unreleased objects in memory	Implement garbage collection, proper memory allocation
Slow API Responses	Overloaded backend, unoptimized requests	Use caching, asynchronous processing
UI Freezing	Blocking the main thread	Use multi-threading, background tasks

Detecting Performance Bottlenecks

cProfile helps analyze which parts of the code are **slow**.

```python
import cProfile

def slow_function():
    total = 0
    for i in range(10**6):
        total += i
    return total

cProfile.run('slow_function()')
```

Identifies slow function calls in Python.

Using dotnet-trace for Profiling in C#

```sh
dotnet-trace collect -p 12345
```

Collects performance traces for .NET applications.

Using Visual Studio Profiler

- **CPU Usage:** Identifies functions consuming high CPU.

- **Memory Analyzer:** Detects memory leaks and excessive allocations.
- **Database Profiler:** Finds slow SQL queries.

Gives a detailed breakdown of resource consumption in C# applications.

17.2 Memory Management in Python and C#

Memory management ensures applications run **efficiently without leaks or excessive usage**.

Memory Management in Python

Python uses **automatic garbage collection (GC)**, but inefficient memory handling can slow applications down.

How Python's Garbage Collector Works

- **Reference Counting:** Objects are deleted when no references exist.
- **Generational Garbage Collection:** Python groups objects into **three generations (young, middle-aged,**

old) and collects garbage **more frequently** in the younger generations.

Optimizing Memory Usage in Python

Manually Trigger Garbage Collection

python

```python
import gc
gc.collect()
```

Use Generators Instead of Lists

python

```python
def large_data():
    for i in range(10**6):
        yield i   # Uses less memory

for item in large_data():
    pass
```

Use NumPy for Large Data Processing

python

```python
import numpy as np
arr = np.array(range(10**6))
```

More memory-efficient than Python lists.

Memory Management in C#

C# uses **automatic garbage collection**, but developers should manage memory efficiently.

Garbage Collection in C#

GC Generation Description

Gen 0   Short-lived objects (frequent collection).

Gen 1   Medium-lived objects.

Gen 2   Long-lived objects (less frequent collection).

Preventing Memory Leaks in C#

Use `Dispose()` to Manually Release Resources

csharp

```
using (var stream = new FileStream("file.txt",
FileMode.Open))
{
    // Use the file
}
```

Use Weak References for Large Objects

csharp

```
WeakReference<string>    weakRef    =    new
WeakReference<string>("LargeString");
```

Avoid Event Handler Memory Leaks

csharp

```
myButton.Click -= Button_Click;
```

Prevents memory leaks caused by unremoved event handlers.

17.3 Load Testing and Stress Testing

Performance testing ensures applications can **handle expected and extreme workloads**.

Test Type	Purpose	Example
Load Testing	Measures application performance under normal load.	Simulating 1,000 concurrent users.
Stress Testing	Tests how an application behaves under extreme load.	Pushing a server beyond its limits.
Soak Testing	Checks system stability over time.	Running an app continuously for 24 hours.
Spike Testing	Tests performance when load suddenly increases.	Simulating flash sales on an e-commerce site.

Load Testing with Apache JMeter

JMeter simulates multiple users accessing an application.

Install JMeter

sh

```
sudo apt install jmeter
```

Run a Load Test
sh

```
jmeter -n -t testplan.jmx -l results.csv
```

Analyzes how many requests per second the application can handle.

Stress Testing with Locust (Python)

Locust allows developers to simulate thousands of concurrent users.

Install Locust
sh

```
pip install locust
```

Create a Load Test Script
python

```
from locust import HttpUser, task

class LoadTest(HttpUser):
    @task
    def test_home(self):
        self.client.get("/")
```

Run the Test

```sh

```

```
locust          -f              load_test.py            --
host=http://localhost:5000
```

Simulates thousands of users accessing the application.

Load Testing in C# with k6

k6 is a load-testing tool for **.NET applications**.

Install k6

```sh

```

```
choco install k6
```

Write a k6 Test Script

```js

```

```
import http from 'k6/http';
import { check } from 'k6';

export default function () {
    let res = http.get('http://localhost:5000');
    check(res, { 'status is 200': (r) => r.status
=== 200 });
}
```

Run the Load Test

sh

```
k6 run test.js
```

Measures how a .NET API performs under high load.

Final Thoughts: Why Performance Optimization Matters?

Identifying bottlenecks improves application speed and efficiency.

Efficient memory management prevents slowdowns and crashes.

Load testing ensures the application scales under heavy usage.

Key Takeaways from This Chapter:

Profiling tools (cProfile, dotnet-trace) help detect performance   bottlenecks.

Memory management techniques improve efficiency in Python   and   C#.

Load and stress testing ensure applications perform well under high traffic.

Next Chapter: We explore **Blockchain and Smart Contracts**, covering **Ethereum, Solidity, and real-world blockchain applications**.

CHAPTER 18

SOFTWARE DEVELOPMENT TRENDS AND THE FUTURE OF MULTI-PLATFORM APPLICATIONS

The **software development landscape** is evolving rapidly, driven by **low-code/no-code platforms, AI-assisted development, and emerging multi-platform technologies**. Businesses and developers must adapt to **faster development cycles, cross-platform demands, and AI-driven automation**. In this chapter, we explore **the rise of low-code/no-code platforms, AI-assisted software development, and predictions for the future of multi-platform applications**.

18.1 The Rise of Low-Code/No-Code Platforms

What Are Low-Code/No-Code Platforms?

Low-code and no-code platforms allow developers (and non-developers) to build applications **visually with minimal coding**.

Feature	Low-Code	No-Code
Target Audience	Developers & IT teams	Business users, non-developers
Customization	Allows custom coding	Limited customization
Speed of Development	Fast (some coding required)	Very fast (drag-and-drop)
Best Use Case	Enterprise apps, workflow automation	Simple web & mobile apps

Popular Low-Code/No-Code Platforms

Platform	Type	Use Case
Microsoft PowerApps	Low-Code	Enterprise workflow automation
OutSystems	Low-Code	Multi-platform business applications

Platform	Type	Use Case
Mendix	Low-Code	AI-driven application development
Bubble	No-Code	Web & mobile apps
Appgyver	No-Code	Cross-platform mobile apps

Advantages of Low-Code/No-Code Development

Faster Time to Market → Build applications in days instead of months.

Reduced Development Costs → Less reliance on software engineers.

Accessibility → Enables **non-technical users** to build applications.

Easy Integration → Connects with existing databases, APIs, and cloud services.

Challenges of Low-Code/No-Code Platforms

Limited Customization → Cannot handle complex logic like traditional programming.

218

Vendor Lock-In $\rightarrow$ Applications are tied to platform-specific services.

Security Risks $\rightarrow$ Less control over backend security and data.

Real-World Example: Low-Code in Action

✦ **Case Study: Siemens Using Mendix**
Siemens, a global industrial company, used **Mendix (a low-code platform)** to build industrial IoT applications. **Results:**

50% faster development time.

Reduced maintenance costs.

Non-developers contributed to app creation.

18.2 AI-Assisted Software Development

AI is transforming software development by **automating coding tasks, optimizing workflows, and enhancing productivity**.

How AI is Changing Software Development

AI Use Case	Impact
AI Code Generation	Writes code based on descriptions (e.g., GitHub Copilot, OpenAI Codex)
Bug Detection	AI-powered tools like **DeepCode** find and fix security vulnerabilities.
Automated Testing	AI generates test cases and automates QA testing.
Code Refactoring	AI improves code efficiency and readability.

Popular AI-Powered Development Tools

Tool	Use Case
GitHub Copilot	AI-assisted coding (suggests code snippets)
Tabnine	AI-powered code completion
DeepCode	AI-based bug detection
Testim	AI-powered automated testing

Tool	Use Case
Amazon CodeWhisperer	AI-assisted programming for AWS projects

Example: AI-Assisted Code Generation with GitHub Copilot

python

```python
# Copilot suggests this code based on a comment
def fibonacci(n):
    if n <= 0:
        return []
    elif n == 1:
        return [0]
    elif n == 2:
        return [0, 1]
    else:
        seq = [0, 1]
        for i in range(2, n):
            seq.append(seq[-1] + seq[-2])
        return seq

print(fibonacci(10))
```

GitHub Copilot generates fully functional code from a comment.

Challenges of AI-Assisted Development

Code Quality Issues → AI-generated code may have **security** **vulnerabilities**.
Over-Reliance on AI → Developers may become less skilled in **problem-solving**.
Ethical Concerns → AI may use code snippets from righted repositories.

Real-World Example: AI-Powered Development

✦ **Case Study: AI-Powered Bug Fixing at Microsoft**
Microsoft used **DeepCode AI** to scan millions of lines of C# code.
Results:
Detected 80% of security vulnerabilities automatically.
Saved thousands of developer hours in bug fixes.

18.3 Predictions for the Future of Multi-Platform Development

The future of multi-platform development is shaped by **AI, cloud computing, blockchain, and emerging programming paradigms**.

Rise of AI-Generated Code

- **AI will write 50% of enterprise code** by 2030 (Gartner Prediction).
- **Low-code AI-assisted platforms** will replace traditional development for business applications.
- **Developers will shift from writing code to designing AI workflows.**

Cross-Platform Development Will Be Dominated by Web Technologies

- **Progressive Web Apps (PWAs)** will replace native mobile apps.
- **WebAssembly (Wasm)** will allow **high-performance apps in the browser**.
- **Flutter and React Native** will dominate multi-platform development.

Future **Tech:**

WebAssembly (Wasm) → Runs compiled code in browsers at near-native speeds.
Blazor WebAssembly → Brings .NET to web applications.
React Native & Flutter → Leading cross-platform frameworks.

Blockchain Will Revolutionize Software Development

- **Decentralized applications (DApps)** will replace traditional web apps.
- **Smart contracts** will automate business logic.
- **Ethereum, Solana, and Hyperledger** will become dominant blockchain platforms.

Cloud-Native and Edge Computing Will Dominate

- **Serverless architectures** will replace traditional backend systems.
- **Edge computing** will power **IoT and AI at the device level**.

- **Multi-cloud development** will be the standard for enterprise applications.

Popular Cloud Services for Multi-Platform Development:

Service	Cloud Provider	Use Case
AWS Lambda	Amazon AWS	Serverless computing
Azure Functions	Microsoft Azure	Event-driven applications
Firebase	Google Cloud	Mobile & web backend services

Final Thoughts: The Future of Software Development

The future is moving towards AI-powered, cloud-native, and low-code development. Multi-platform applications will rely more on web technologies and blockchain integration. Developers will shift from writing code to designing AI-powered workflows.

225

Key Takeaways from This Chapter:

Low-code/no-code platforms are speeding up development.

AI is transforming coding with intelligent assistants.
Blockchain, cloud, and WebAssembly are shaping the future of multi-platform development.

Conclusion: This book has covered **building, optimizing, and securing multi-platform applications using Python, C#, and modern software development trends**.

CHAPTER 19

CASE STUDIES: REAL-WORLD MULTI-PLATFORM APPLICATIONS

Understanding real-world case studies provides valuable insights into the challenges and success strategies of building **multi-platform applications**. In this chapter, we explore **successful stories** of companies using **Python and C#** for cross-platform development, **lessons from failed projects**, and **best practices for long-term software maintenance**.

19.1 Success Stories of Companies Using Python and C#

Spotify - Python for Backend, C# for Desktop Application

Spotify, a leading **music streaming service**, uses **Python** extensively in its backend for **data processing, machine learning**, and **real-time analytics**. Additionally, **C#** is used for the **Spotify desktop application**, making it possible to run seamlessly on **Windows and macOS**.

Challenges

- Need for **fast, scalable backend** capable of handling millions of requests.
- Building a **cross-platform** desktop app for users across multiple operating systems.

Solutions

- **Python with Celery and Kafka** was used for handling large-scale data processing and communication between services.
- **C# with .NET Core** ensured that the desktop app could easily run on **Windows** and **macOS**, offering a native experience on both platforms.

Results

Python's scalability helped Spotify manage millions of concurrent   users.
C# desktop app provided users with a smooth, consistent experience on multiple platforms.

228

Microsoft Teams - C# for Cross-Platform Collaboration

Microsoft Teams, a popular **collaboration tool**, leverages C# and **.NET Core** to run on **Windows, macOS, Linux, iOS, and Android**. The app integrates seamlessly with Microsoft Office 365, making it a powerful tool for business collaboration.

Challenges

- Need for **cross-platform compatibility** while ensuring tight integration with **Office 365**.
- High demands for **real-time communication** and **multimedia support** across platforms.

Solutions

- **C# with .NET Core** was used to ensure the application could run on multiple operating systems, maintaining performance and security.
- **SignalR (C#)** was used to ensure real-time communication in the app.

Results

C# and .NET Core allowed **Teams** to be deployed on all platforms, providing users with a unified experience. **Real-time communication** was achieved through **SignalR**, improving user engagement and collaboration.

Dropbox - Python for Backend, C++ for Syncing

Dropbox, a cloud storage service, utilizes **Python** for backend development and **C++** for its **sync engine** to ensure quick synchronization of files across platforms.

Challenges

- Need for efficient **file synchronization** across **multiple devices**.
- Handling **large-scale data** storage and retrieval, while maintaining **cross-platform compatibility**.

Solutions

- **Python** powered the backend, managing user accounts and handling file metadata.

- **C++** was used for the **sync engine** due to its performance in processing file transfers and updates across different platforms.

Results

Python streamlined Dropbox's backend logic, while **C++** allowed efficient file synchronization on all platforms. Dropbox became one of the **most widely used cloud storage services** worldwide.

19.2 Lessons from Failed Multi-Platform Projects

Windows 8 - C# with WinRT

Microsoft's Windows 8 attempted to create a universal platform for both **desktop** and **tablet/mobile devices**. The goal was to use **C# and WinRT** for a unified platform across devices. However, the project faced several challenges.

Challenges

- **Windows 8's UI design** was poorly received by users, as it was optimized for touchscreens but not for traditional desktop users.

- **WinRT API limitations** made it difficult to achieve full cross-platform compatibility across all types of Windows devices.

Lessons Learned

- **User Experience (UX)** is key when developing cross-platform applications.
- **A unified design for different devices** (e.g., desktop and mobile) requires careful consideration of user interaction across platforms.
- **API compatibility** is critical for ensuring seamless experience across all devices.

Google Glass - Android & C++ Integration

Google Glass, the wearable smart device, was initially built on **Android and C++**, but it failed to achieve mass adoption.

Challenges

- **Limited app ecosystem** and difficulty in developing **cross-platform apps** for both the device and Android.
- **Battery life and performance issues** arose due to the hardware limitations of the device.

Lessons Learned

- **Hardware limitations** should be considered when building apps for new devices, especially for wearables.
- A **strong app ecosystem** is essential to drive user adoption for a new platform.
- **Cross-platform integration** can be complex, requiring better developer support and unified tools.

19.3 Best Practices for Long-Term Software Maintenance

To ensure the longevity of multi-platform applications, **software maintenance** is essential. This includes **regular updates**, **bug fixes**, and adapting to **new platforms** and technologies.

Use Cross-Platform Frameworks

Frameworks like **Flutter**, **React Native**, **Xamarin**, and **.NET MAUI** help in maintaining a **single codebase** that can be deployed across multiple platforms. This ensures that updates and bug fixes are easier to manage.

Example:

- **Flutter** allows the same codebase to run on **iOS, Android, Windows, macOS,** and even **web**.
- **.NET MAUI** extends **Xamarin** to support more platforms, such as **macOS** and **Windows**.

Modular Code Architecture

Building applications in a **modular way** makes it easier to manage and update specific parts of the codebase. This **separation of concerns** improves maintainability by reducing complexity and ensuring faster bug fixes.

Example:

- A **modularized codebase** with **clear boundaries** for user interface, business logic, and data management ensures easier updates and troubleshooting.

Regular Code Refactoring

Over time, codebases grow and can become harder to maintain. **Refactoring** involves restructuring existing code to improve its design and maintainability, without changing its functionality.

Best Practice:

- **Code reviews** and **refactoring sprints** should be scheduled regularly to ensure the code remains clean and maintainable.

Automated Testing and Continuous Integration

Maintaining a **robust automated testing suite** ensures that every change made to the application does not break existing functionality.

Best Practice:

- Implement **CI/CD pipelines** (e.g., using **Jenkins, GitHub Actions**) to automate testing and deployments.
- Use **unit tests**, **integration tests**, and **UI tests** to catch issues early.

Documentation and Knowledge Sharing

Comprehensive **documentation** is essential for long-term maintainability, especially for multi-platform applications that involve different frameworks and technologies. Regular **knowledge sharing** among team members is key.

Best Practice:

- Use tools like **Swagger/OpenAPI** for API documentation and maintain **internal wikis** for code standards and architecture.

Final Thoughts: Real-World Successes and Failures

Successes: Companies like **Spotify, Microsoft Teams, and Dropbox** have shown that combining the right technologies (Python and C#) with **cross-platform strategies** leads to scalable, high-performing applications. **Failures**: Projects like **Windows 8** and **Google Glass** highlight the importance of **user experience, hardware considerations, and ecosystem development** in cross-platform development.

Key Takeaways from This Chapter:

Successful multi-platform projects rely on a unified codebase, scalable architecture, and effective cross-platform frameworks.

Lessons from failures remind us of the importance of **user**

experience and **compatibility across devices**. **Long-term maintenance** requires **modular architectures**, **automated testing**, and **regular refactoring**.

Next Chapter: We explore **Software Architecture and Design Patterns** for multi-platform development, focusing on **MVC, MVVM, and microservices architectures**.

CHAPTER 20

CONCLUSION AND NEXT STEPS FOR DEVELOPERS

As multi-platform development continues to grow, **developers are presented with exciting opportunities** to work on diverse and scalable applications. Whether you are a beginner or an experienced developer, learning to build, optimize, and deploy cross-platform applications using **Python, C#, and other modern tools** is a valuable skillset for the future. In this final chapter, we will discuss **building a career in multi-platform development**, **expanding your skillset**, and **recommended learning resources** to help you stay ahead in this ever-evolving field.

20.1 Building a Career in Multi-Platform Development

Why Choose Multi-Platform Development?

As businesses strive to provide seamless experiences across multiple devices and platforms, the demand for **multi-platform developers** has skyrocketed. Multi-platform

development offers several key advantages:
Wide Reach: Ability to build apps for **web, desktop, and mobile**.

Scalability: Develop applications that scale across various operating systems and devices.

Versatility: Work on diverse projects across industries like **gaming, finance, healthcare, and e-commerce**.

Essential Skills for a Multi-Platform Developer

Strong Foundation in Programming

- Learn core languages like **Python** and **C#** for backend and application development.
- Master cross-platform frameworks such as **Flutter**, **React Native**, and **.NET MAUI** for building apps.

Understanding of APIs and Cloud Services

- Learn how to build and consume **REST APIs** and integrate with cloud platforms like **AWS**, **Azure**, and **Google Cloud**.
- Understand **serverless architectures** and **microservices** for scalable backend services.

UI/UX Design Knowledge

- Understand design principles for creating **responsive user interfaces** across mobile, web, and desktop applications.
- Familiarize yourself with UI frameworks like **Qt, Kivy**, and **XAML**.

Knowledge of Testing and DevOps

- Master **unit testing, integration testing**, and **CI/CD pipelines** for efficient, error-free development.
- Learn **DevOps practices** and tools like **Docker** and **Kubernetes** for containerization and deployment.

20.2 Expanding Your Skillset in Python, C#, and Beyond

Deepening Your Python and C# Expertise

Both **Python** and **C#** are powerful tools for cross-platform development, and mastering these languages will open doors to a wide range of opportunities.

Python

- **Focus on Machine Learning and AI:** Learn libraries like **TensorFlow**, **Scikit-learn**, and **PyTorch** to build AI-powered applications.

- **Web Development:** Get hands-on experience with frameworks like **Flask** and **Django** for creating scalable web applications.
- **Automation and Scripting:** Master Python's strengths in **automation**, **scripting**, and **data processing** for various industries.

C#

- **.NET Core for Web and Desktop Apps:** Dive into **ASP.NET Core** for building **web applications** and **.NET MAUI** for cross-platform desktop apps.
- **Game Development with Unity:** Learn **Unity** for creating **cross-platform games** and interactive experiences.
- **Cloud and Azure Development:** Get certified in **Azure development** and focus on building **cloud-native apps** with **C#**.

Beyond Python and C#: Exploring New Technologies

To stay relevant in multi-platform development, consider expanding your skillset into these key areas:

Mobile Development with React Native and Flutter

- **React Native** and **Flutter** enable the creation of **cross-platform mobile apps** with a **single codebase**, ensuring faster development and broader reach.

WebAssembly (Wasm) and Progressive Web Apps (PWAs)

- **WebAssembly** allows developers to write code in **C#, C++, Rust**, and other languages that runs in the browser at near-native speeds.
- **PWAs** allow you to build **web apps that function like native mobile apps**, offering a new path for cross-platform development.

Blockchain and Smart Contracts

- **Blockchain** development with **Ethereum** and **Solidity** offers new opportunities for **decentralized applications (DApps)** and **smart contracts**.

Cloud Technologies and Serverless Computing

- Master **serverless architectures** with platforms like **AWS Lambda**, **Azure Functions**, and **Google Cloud Functions** to build scalable and efficient applications.

20.3 Final Thoughts and Recommended Learning Resources

As **multi-platform development** continues to evolve, the key to success lies in **continuous learning** and adapting to new technologies. Whether you focus on improving your skills in Python and C# or explore **new tools and platforms**, staying up-to-date is essential for building **high-quality applications**.

Recommended Learning Resources

Books:

- **"Fluent Python"** by Luciano Ramalho - A deep dive into Python.
- **"Pro ASP.NET Core 3"** by Adam Freeman - A complete guide to building scalable web apps with C#.
- **"Clean Code"** by Robert C. Martin - A must-read for improving coding practices.

Online Courses:

- **Udemy**: Offers comprehensive courses on **Flutter, React Native**, and **C#**.
- **Coursera**: Courses on **AI, Cloud Computing**, and **Machine Learning**.

243

- **Pluralsight**: Advanced courses on **.NET Core**, **Azure**, and **Cross-Platform Development**.

Communities and Forums:

- **Stack Overflow** - A go-to resource for troubleshooting coding issues.
- **GitHub** - Contribute to open-source projects and collaborate with other developers.
- **Reddit (r/learnprogramming, r/csharp)** - Engage with fellow learners and professionals.

Next Steps

Start a personal project to apply your multi-platform development skills. Build something that spans across **web, mobile, and desktop platforms** to get hands-on experience. **Contribute to open-source projects** to learn from others and showcase your skills. **Stay updated** by following blogs, podcasts, and attending tech conferences focused on **cross-platform development**.

Key Takeaways from This Chapter:

Building a career in multi-platform development requires continuous learning and mastering core programming languages like **Python and C#**. **Expanding your skillset** through frameworks like **Flutter, React Native**, and exploring **emerging technologies** will keep you ahead in the industry. **Recommended learning resources** such as books, online courses, and community involvement will support your growth as a multi-platform developer.

Good luck on your journey! Keep coding, keep learning, and stay innovative as you build the future of **multi-platform applications**.